Praying God's Will for Your Life

WORKBOOK AND JOURNAL

STORMIE OMARTIAN

Praying God's Will for Your Life

WORKBOOK AND JOURNAL

A Personal Prayer Walk to Spiritual Well-Being

STORMIE OMARTIAN

THOMAS NELSON
Since 1798

NASHVILLE   DALLAS   MEXICO CITY   RIO DE JANEIRO

Contents

PART ONE

The Intimate Relationship

CHAPTER ONE

Praying to Know God's Will for Your Life

WHEN I BECAME A CHRISTIAN, I WANTED TO KNOW GOD'S WILL FOR my life. And when I had children, I wanted the same for them as well. I prayed that my son, Chris, and my daughter, Mandy, would also know and follow God's will. Growing up the way I did, being so far out of the will of God, I knew the mistakes that can be made when you don't walk with the Lord. It almost ruined my life, and it took years to get on the right track.

My spiritually adopted son, John, didn't come to be with our family until he was sixteen, after his dad was killed in a car accident. His mom, Diane, who had been my closest friend for twenty-eight years, had died of cancer when John was only eight. The week he was born, Diane and her husband had asked me if I would take care of him if anything ever happened to them. Of course, I said yes, and John was left to us in their will. A week before Diane died she had asked me again, and I assured her I would always take care of him.

While Diane was alive, she and I prayed that her beloved son would know the will of God. And after his mom and dad died, I began praying fervently for him in that way too. In the next two years John faced major decisions, the most important being which college he should attend. He got a full scholarship to every college he applied to, including Vanderbilt, and I couldn't help but wish that he would stay in Tennessee so he could be close to us. But he felt that God was leading him to go to a university in the state of Washington, so that was the decision he made.

I then began praying that he would find the perfect wife. When John came to visit us during the summer after his sophomore year, he showed me a little book of poems and writings that his girlfriend, Rebecca, had made for him so that a part of her could go with him during the weeks they were separated. He let me read it, and as I read I fell in love with her too. The writings were so insightful, intelligent, creative. *What an exceptional girl,* I thought. *When I meet her I hope I love her as much as I love what she's written.*

At the end of that summer Rebecca came to spend a week with us, and our whole family realized that this was the girl God had chosen for John. Her writing was an accurate extension of her spirit. Tears came to my eyes as I realized how much John's mom and dad would have loved her as well. She was everything anyone would want in a daughter-in-law.

John once wondered if he should have gone to Vanderbilt because he said he missed being with us when he was so far away at college. But after he met Rebecca we all knew it was the right decision; he had followed the will of God. Our prayers had been answered.

Throughout life we all face decisions that require God's guidance. And so do the people we care about. We must pray for ourselves—and for our loved ones—so that we will all understand what the will of God is for our lives.

A TURNING POINT

I had been a singer and an actress on television for about three years when I was asked to sing on a series of recording sessions for a Christian musical. I wasn't a Christian so I had no idea what one was. My friend Terry was the contractor on this session, which meant she was in charge of hiring all the singers. She was one of the best studio singers in Los Angeles, and I had worked with her often. She always sang the lead, and I would stand next to her and sing second.

On our lunch break we went out together in a large group, and I learned that everyone on the session was a Christian except me. They all talked about their futures, some of which seemed to be even more precarious than mine. Yet none of them feared the future as I did. They said that God had a plan for their lives and as long as they walked in the will of God, their futures were secure in His hands. I had never heard of such a thing.

Each day of the sessions I found myself increasingly attracted to the sense of purpose these people had. *I wonder if God has a plan for my life?* I thought to myself. That would mean I didn't have to make life happen. I thought about this for the next few days of the sessions. And I tried to learn more from each of the singers at every lunch break without letting them know why I was interested. I didn't want anyone pressuring me to have a life of purpose.

As I was on my way home from the last session on the final day, I prayed to this God of theirs without knowing if He could even hear me. "God, if You have a will for my life," I said, "I need to know what it is and what to do about it."

I heard no reply. As I suspected, this God would probably never listen to someone like me. Yet over the course of the next few months many things happened to me, one of which changed my life forever: I met the God that Terry and her friends had been talking about. The simple prayer I had prayed in the car, to a God I didn't even know, was answered.

That was thirty-two years ago, and now I know that the will of God is not some mysterious thing that only a few select people can understand. It's there for each one of us, but we have to take the necessary steps to find it. The steps are simple, but often for that very reason we don't bother to take them.

Ultimately God's will for us is to make us more like Christ. That's His goal, and He has a plan for each step of this process. This simplifies everything because we don't have to figure it all out and make it all happen. We just have to look to the Lord, knowing *He* has it all figured out and *He* will make it happen.

As we begin our journey in this workbook to find God's will for each day of our lives, we need to be aware of four important aspects of His will. *The first and most important is that His will is most often found by reading the Bible.* The Bible declares clearly that God does have a definite will for each of our lives. Psalm 37:23 says, "The steps of a good man are ordered by the LORD." And in Psalm 32:8, God promises, "I will instruct you and teach you in the way you should go." He speaks to us through His Word in the Scriptures.

Second, God's will is continuous. From the time we are infants until the day we die, God has a will for us—as children, young people, adults, and senior citizens. Isaiah 58:11:

The LORD will guide you continually,
And satisfy your soul in drought,
And strengthen your bones;
You shall be like a watered garden,
And like a spring of water, whose waters do not fail.

Third, God's will is specific. The prophet Isaiah heard the Lord promising His children, "Your ears shall hear a word behind you, saying, 'This is the way, walk in it,' whenever you turn to the right hand or whenever you turn to the left" (Isaiah 30:21).

And finally, God's will is profitable. The Lord told Joshua who was to lead the Israelites into the Promised Land: "This Book of the Law shall not depart from your mouth, but you shall meditate in it day and night, that you may observe to do according to all that is written in it. *For then you will make your way prosperous, and then you will have good success*" (Joshua 1:8, emphasis added).

In the days after I became a Christian I continually prayed, *God, tell me what to do. Show me what steps to take. Guide me where I need to go.* And God answered those prayers. He spoke to my heart, saying, *Just be in My presence. I'll make things happen the way they are supposed to.*

In the following months and years I learned that life could be much simpler than I ever dreamed. It didn't matter what my situation was at the moment; all I had to do was take the next step the Lord was showing me. As I did, I began to see a solid way of living that I could easily explain to other people. I would say, "You just take these steps. As long as you are walking with God and living His way, you are not likely to get off the path. And if by chance you do, He will get you right back on. That's because you've been listening to God's voice. You will feel in your heart when you violate one of His directions." I will explain this in greater depth as we progress through this book.

This book is divided into three parts, which represent our overall goals in the process of finding God's will for our lives:

- to establish an intimate relationship with God (The Intimate Relationship),
- to lay a solid foundation in His truth (The Solid Foundation), and
- to learn the basic principles of obedience (The Obedient Walk).

All of these things are the will of God for our lives, as revealed in His Word, and we must do them in order to be in His will. I worked readers through these goals and the steps toward attaining them in my book *Praying God's Will for Your Life*. This book is a Bible study of the twenty-two steps from that book. It will give you the chance to personalize these steps and deepen your walk with God.

Throughout the chapters you will find interactive exercises so that you can apply each step to your particular situation. You will also have an opportunity to grow in your prayer life with the Lord as you write prayers that ask God to walk with you through each step. And at the end of the book there is a prayer journal so that you can continue to record your prayers—and watch for answers.

At the end of each chapter are Scriptures that will help you further understand and build on your knowledge of that particular step. Writing the Scripture passages in this book helps you to compare them and easily refer to the teaching later on. You can work through the material on your own, or you can use it for a Bible study or home-cell group or as a Sunday-school curriculum.

As you end this chapter, take a moment to think about your life. What do you think God's will is for you during the next week? Write that in the space below:

What is His will for you in the next month?

In the next year?

Five years from now?

Ultimately His will for you is to make you more like His Son, Jesus Christ. The center of God's will is not a destination; it's a process. And that process begins this week and continues into next month and next year and five years from today—and for the rest of your life.

Now let me tell you about each of these steps and how I learned of their importance in our lives.

GOD'S WILL FOR YOUR LIFE

Scripture is very clear that God has a will for each of our lives. Look up the passages below and write them in the space provided.

Ephesians 2:20

This passage says that we are _____.

Created to do _____.

And when did God prepare this plan for us?

Hebrews 12:1

Who surrounds us?

Think about that. Each day we are supported by _____.

And our goal for each day is _____.

Psalm 1:1–3

The promises in this Scripture for those who delight in the law of the Lord are:

CHAPTER TWO

Praying to Know God as a Powerful Presence

A FEW MONTHS AFTER THE SERIES OF RECORDING SESSIONS, MY friend Terry said, "I can see you're not doing well, Stormie. Won't you come with me and talk to my pastor?" Sensing my reluctance, she quickly added, "You've got nothing to lose."

I silently bore witness to her accurate assessment of my situation and agreed to go even though I wanted nothing whatsoever to do with any kind of religion. My experience with churches had been that they made me feel deader than I did already.

Terry took me to meet Pastor Jack Hayford from the nearby Church on the Way, and it turned out to be like no other meeting I'd ever had. I had no trouble listening to him talk about God because I knew there was a spirit realm. I had seen enough supernatural manifestations through my delving into the occult to convince me of their reality. But when he started talking about receiving Jesus and being born again, I was interested but cautious.

Fortunately, Pastor Jack saw through my fears and didn't push me for any commitment. Instead he sent me home with three books. One of those books was *The Screwtape Letters* by C. S. Lewis, a classic about the reality of evil. Since I had been into the occult and was familiar with this territory, I'm sure Pastor felt that this book would appeal to me.

The book is a compilation of letters from Screwtape, a senior devil, to his nephew, Wormwood, in which Screwtape instructs this junior devil on the art of temptation. As we make our journey throughout this workbook and journal, I will use excerpts from these letters to help us see our mistakes (for what pleases Screwtape is not likely to please the Lord).

Unfortunately people tend to reject the thought of a real devil who is active in our modern world. In *The Screwtape Letters*, Screwtape instructs Wormwood to take advantage of this human disbelief in the war between good and evil. "Our policy, for the moment," he says, "is to conceal ourselves." He goes on to assure Wormwood:

> I do not think you will have much difficulty in keeping the patient [Wormwood's human charge] in the dark. The fact that devils are predominantly *comic* figures in the modern imagination will help you. If any faint suspicion of your existence begins to arise in his mind, suggest to him a picture of something in red tights, and persuade him that since he cannot believe in that (it is an old textbook method of confusing them) he therefore cannot believe in you.[1]

As I read *The Screwtape Letters*, I saw that my New Age belief—that there is no evil in the world except what exists in people's minds—was a deception. There is an evil force intent on our destruction, and Satan, the head of that force, *is* real and very much our enemy. Suddenly it all made sense.

The Bible clearly testifies to the reality of evil. Zechariah, an Old Testament prophet, had a vision in which he clearly saw Satan opposing Joshua, the high priest: "Then he showed me Joshua the high priest standing before the Angel of the Lord, and Satan standing at his right hand to oppose him" (Zechariah 3:1).

And Jesus Himself was tempted by Satan just before the Lord began His ministry: "And immediately the Spirit drove Him into the wilderness. And He was there in the wilderness forty days, tempted by Satan, and was with the wild beasts; and the angels ministered to Him" (Mark 1:12–13).

Satan is alive and well throughout the Old and New Testaments of the Bible, and unfortunately he is alive and well in the world today.

Another book Pastor Jack gave me was the gospel of John in book form, and it changed my life. I will refer to it along with other books of the Bible as we walk through this journey together. The Scriptures will guide us on our path and are crucial to our spiritual life.

THE MOST IMPORTANT STEP YOU'LL EVER TAKE

All of us need to acknowledge God, recognize that He is on our side, and let Him be Lord over our lives.

The prophet Jeremiah asked God a question we all ask: "Why then is there no healing for the wound of my people?" (Jeremiah 8:22 NIV).

And God answered, "They go from one sin to another; they do not acknowledge me" (Jeremiah 9:3 NIV).

One of the main reasons people are lonely and distressed is that they have not taken five important steps in having an intimate relationship with God. They have not acknowledged God

- as Savior,
- as Father,
- as Holy Spirit,
- as Lord in every area of life, or
- as the Name who answers their every need.

In this first part of the workbook, let's look at each of these steps that lead to an intimate relationship with God.

God is composed of three different aspects: the Father, the Son, and the Holy Spirit. Three parts, but only one God. That can be difficult to understand until you think about your own life. You may be a wife, a mother, and an employee—three different functions or aspects—but only one person: You. You are able to be all three at one time. So is God.

If you have never acknowledged God's presence in your life, write a short prayer in the space at the top of the next page, asking God to show you any way you have failed to acknowledge His presence in your life and asking Him to help you sense His presence in the future.

In the next week be aware of God's presence in your life and when you sense it in specific ways, record those moments in the space below:

As you look for these times, ask yourself:

- Did I feel God's presence in the activities of my day?
- In the love and concern of a friend?
- In the face of a child?
- In a moment when I prayed to Him?
- When I looked at the beauty of His creation?
- When I read the Bible?

If you are already aware of God's presence in your life, you may want to renew your commitment to Him. Write a short prayer in the space below, acknowledging Him again in this way and asking Him to help you sense His hand on you as you go about your daily tasks. End by thanking Him for His love and care for you.

Can you think of a special time when you sensed God's presence in your life in the past? Record that moment in the space below:

Proverbs 3:6 says "In all your ways acknowledge Him, and He shall direct your paths." During the next few days, use the space below to make note of the different ways you can acknowledge God's presence in your life.

God makes this promise to you: "I am with you always, even to the end of the age" (Matthew 28:20).

ASPECTS OF GOD WHEN THE HEBREW WORD IS *ELOHIM*

The word *Elohim*, which is the plural form of the Hebrew word for "majesty," is translated "God" 2,570 times in the Old Testament.[2] I have listed the different aspects of God below and the passages that tell about this aspect. Look up the passages and write them in the spaces below each Scripture. Then write what this aspect of God means to you.

CREATOR

John 1:1–3

When I see God as Creator, I think of _____.

THE LIGHT

John 1:9

When I see God as the Light, I feel _____.

Is there an area in your life where you need to see God as your Light? If so, explain.

PERSONAL GOD

Genesis 48:15

When I see God as personal to me, I feel _____.

Is there an area in your life where you need to see Him in this way? If so, explain in the space below:

Read Psalm 23 and note the aspects of God that are most meaningful to you.

When I see God in these ways, I know _____.

Is there an area in your life where you need to see Him in this way? If so, write that area in the space below:

ASPECTS OF GOD WHEN THE HEBREW WORD IS *ELOAH*

The word *Eloah,* a singular form of *Elohim,* is also used for God in the Old Testament.[3] I have listed two different aspects of God below and the passages that tell about this aspect. Look up the passages and write them in the spaces below each Scripture. Then write what this aspect of God means to you.

A SHIELD

Proverbs 30:5

When I see God as my shield, I _____.

Is there an area in your life where you need to see Him in this way? If so, explain in the space below:

A JUDGE

Read Psalm 50:1–6, and note the aspects that are most meaningful to you.

When I see God as a judge, I _____.

Is there an area in your life where you need to see Him in this way? If so, explain in the space below:

CHAPTER THREE

Praying to Know God as Your Savior

I FIRST MET RICH MULLINS, THE WELL-KNOWN CHRISTIAN SINGER, at a meeting of Christian artists. At the time I was struck with how deeply humble he was. Everyone was talking, but Rich seemed quiet—not aloof, just peaceful. As I observed him that day, I saw that the spirit of God was very evident in his life. At the time I didn't know much about him, except that he had written "Awesome God," which is one of my favorite worship songs. It wasn't until later that I learned the details of his life—and how integral his belief in Jesus was to everything he did.

A LIFE TRANSFORMED BY JESUS

When Rich Mullins registered as a student at Friends University, some people wondered if the new arrival was a homeless person because of his well-worn jeans, threadbare sneakers, and long, stringy hair. However, others recognized Mullins as the famous Christian singer. *Why was he enrolling in Friends to get a music education degree?* many wondered. They later learned the answer: so he could teach music to Native American youth on a reservation in New Mexico.

After he graduated from Friends, Mullins did exactly that. He lived in a sheet-metal trailer as he taught music to Navajo children at a Christian school that previously had no music program, no instruments, and no instructor. He also performed concerts for inmates at a nearby jail.

"A lot of people think I've come here to save the Indians," he said when reporters asked him about this change in lifestyle, "but it was a desire [for me] to feel God's love out of the American mainstream."[1] He saw his musical tours as a way to fund his work with the Navajo.

Rich grew up in the former Quaker settlement of Arba, Indiana, where about half the residents were his relatives. He began his music career in his late twenties when his uncle loaned him $1,000 to make an album, which came into the hands of Amy Grant, who was caught by the song "Sing Your Praise to the Lord." Amy recorded the song, which earned Rich Mullins a Dove Award nomination; soon Rich was performing with Grant and recording for Reunion Records.

Toward the end of his career Rich made hundreds of thousands of dollars, yet he lived on $24,000 a year, choosing to give the rest away. He told his accountant not to tell him how much money he had. It was easier to give it away if he didn't know that.[1]

All of Rich's decisions were based on his belief in Jesus and on Rich's love for the Lord. "Christianity is about a daily walk with this person Jesus," he often said. "Life and living comes from God—it comes from Jesus—not from doctrine or good morals."[2]

Rich had it right; it's as simple as that. We need to acknowledge Jesus as Savior and live the way He asks us to live.

As I read the books Pastor Jack gave me, I immediately saw two reasons to acknowledge Jesus as Savior: (1) to be completely free of guilt and (2) to know that your future is secure.

To Be Completely Free of Guilt

If you glance up at the scales of justice in a United States courtroom, you will see that they are held by a blindfolded woman. The symbolism here is evident: Justice is not to be swayed by the appearance of the person who stands before her. Only the facts count. If the evidence tips the scales one way, the person on trial is innocent. However, if the evidence swings the other way, the suspect is guilty. It's that direct, that simple, and that final. And the conviction is, hopefully, always based on fact. Too often, people who are guilty declare themselves to be innocent. And there are some of us who are innocent yet we are always feeling we are guilty.

False Guilt

At one time my own sense of guilt was overwhelming, for all the wrong reasons. My mother had a way of convincing me that everything I did was wrong. As a child I believed her. And it was hard to change that belief in adulthood. After all, my mother had often locked me in a small closet under our stairs for reasons I never understood. I thought I must deserve this extreme punishment. Even though I later realized that she was mentally ill, I still believed that all the negative things she said about me were accurate.

How about you? Do you feel guilty? Before you answer a definite no, consider the statements below and check the ones that describe you:

_____ You have a hard time accepting compliments because you feel don't deserve them.

_____ You have difficulty saying no to people, so you agree to commitments that you really don't want to do.

_____ You feel trapped in an unhealthy relationship because you feel guilty about ending it.

_____ You feel that loss or punishment might be just around the corner.

If you checked several of the statements above, you need to ask yourself, "What might I feel guilty about?"

If you have trouble answering this question, try completing the following sentences:

If only I'd _____.

If I just hadn't _____.

I'm sorry I treated _____ that way.

All of us need to dismiss guilty feelings over things that aren't our fault, but we fear *might* be. For instance, "If I'd been more obedient, maybe my dad wouldn't have left us." This thought kindles false guilt. We blame ourselves for our parents' divorces.

Can you think of anything that causes you to have guilty feelings? List those things here, even though you may suspect that you are wrong to feel this way:

The guilt from these feelings piles up to become a burden that is literally unbearable. And there is no real reason for this guilt.

True Guilt

The second kind of guilt is true guilt. Many of us feel guilty about things we've done that have violated God's laws, some of which we weren't even aware of at the time. This might be the way we have treated a husband or child, or it might be an adulterous affair or an abortion. Whatever the reason, God wants us to be free of it.

Rich Mullins was truly God's messenger of love and hope to many of us. And some thought of him as a spiritual icon. Yet he openly admitted his sins and failings. Rich saw sin as something that must be brought into the light in order to be healed, rather than kept in the darkness. "I've been in and out of all kinds of things," he said, "like self-depreciation, self-interest, ego trips, alcohol, and other addictions."[3]

One day Rich assessed his life and admitted to these secret sins. "I remember being on the road to Michigan and saying to myself, 'Oh, God, why don't you just make my car crash?'"[4]

What or who could take guilt like this away?

Rich Mullins found the answer that day on the road to Michigan. Only God's forgiveness, through our Savior, Jesus Christ.

Instead of his car crashing, he steered the car in the direction of Cincinnati to unburden his soul to a couple of good friends. "It was really liberating," he said. "My struggles with addictions and the darkness I was feeling lessened. There was a renewed feeling of intimacy with God."[5]

In his music and as he spoke to people throughout the United States, Rich Mullins said that no matter how badly we feel about ourselves, we are never unworthy of God's love. "Anytime that we focus on our performance, that in itself cuts us off from God—not successfully—because God's grace is greater than even our darkest sin," he said. "From my junior year of high school until age thirty I felt tormented all the time. I was depressed. I just think I have that sort of personality. Was I going to be kept from the Kingdom of God because I have a tendency to be morose? Or because you have a withered hand? Or because maybe you have some kind of chemical imbalance that leads to an addiction? You're not a Christian because of how you feel, you're a Christian because of what Jesus did for you."[6]

Your Savior, Jesus Christ, died on a cross so your sins could be forgiven. The debt has been canceled.

James Bryan Smith, author of *Rich Mullins: An Arrow Pointing to Heaven* and an assistant professor of theology and university chaplain at Friends University, said, "Through Rich I learned this important truth: If you sin don't hide it; don't be afraid. Rich made it clear that he was no sinless saint. He was honest and direct because he trusted in the unfailing love of God. As a result of his influence, I'm less likely to hide and am more prone to be real. I'm not shocked by my own sinfulness or that of those around me. I now refuse to let sin have the last word."[7]

If you are willing to accept Jesus' gift of forgiveness, say the prayer below:

Jesus, I am sorry for the sins I have committed. I give them to You and promise to do better in the future. Forgive me for not living Your way. I am deeply sorry.

Now that you have said this prayer, read the Scripture below, filling in your name for the blank that has been added to this verse. Hear the Lord, Jesus Christ, saying these words personally to you:

"Come now, and let us reason together,"
Says the LORD.
"Though your sins, _____, are like scarlet,
They shall be white as snow." (Isaiah 1:18)

The second reason to receive Jesus is to have the peace of knowing that your future is secure.

TO KNOW THAT YOUR FUTURE IS SECURE

Nicodemus, a Pharisee and a member of the Sanhedrin, the ruling Jewish council, was one of the first people to accept Jesus' gift of eternal life. Nicodemus had heard about Jesus and knew about the Lord's signs and wonders. "Your miraculous signs are proof enough that God is with you," he told the Lord one night when he met with Jesus secretly.

Nicodemus must have been surprised by the Lord's reply to his statement. Jesus said, "The truth is, no one can enter the Kingdom of God without being born of water and the Spirit."

This concept was truly foreign to Nicodemus. "How can an old man go back into his mother's womb and be born again?" he asked.

Jesus replied, "Humans can reproduce only human life, but the Holy Spirit gives new life from heaven" (John 3:2–6 NLT).

Then Jesus spoke the words that Sunday school students of all faiths memorize: "For God so loved the world that he gave his only Son, so that everyone who believes in him will not perish but have eternal life. God did not send his Son into the world to condemn it, but to save it" (John 3:16–17 NLT).

Later Jesus told His disciples:

> For I have come down from heaven, not to do My own will, but the will of Him who sent Me.
>
> This is the will of the Father who sent Me, that of all He has given Me I should lose nothing, but should raise it up at the last day.
>
> And this is the will of Him who sent Me, that everyone who sees the Son and believes in Him may have everlasting life: and I will raise him up at the last day. (John 6:38–40)

The Lord, Jesus Christ, is speaking this promise directly to you, just as He spoke it to His disciples.

If you are willing to accept this gift, say the prayer at the top of the next page:

Jesus, I acknowledge You this day. I believe You are the Son of God as You say You are. Although it's hard to comprehend love so great, I believe You laid down Your life for me so that I might have life eternally and abundantly now. I need You to help me become all You created me to be. Come into my life and fill me with Your Holy Spirit. Let all the death in me be crowded out by the power of Your presence, and this day turn my life into a new beginning.

Now sign your name below and record your spiritual birth date:

_____   _____ (date)

If you wish to take this moment to renew your commitment to your Savior, write a prayer in the space below. Thank Him for His presence in your life. Acknowledge that you know He is there because you have accepted Him as Savior. And ask Him to help you make a new commitment to living His way.

You are never born again by chance. When you receive Jesus, it is because God the Father is drawing you in. Jesus said, "No one can come to Me unless the Father who sent Me draws him" (John 6:44). Once God draws you in, it's done—once and for all. You are released from guilt, your future is secure, and you are saved from death in every part of your life.

The Scripture doesn't record Nicodemus's response to Jesus' invitation to be born again. But we know that he believed what Jesus told him that day by the way his life changed thereafter. The man who was afraid to be seen with Jesus later defended Him when He was brought before the Sanhedrin. In front of this Jewish high council, which was obviously out to destroy Jesus, Nicodemus asked, "Is it legal to convict a man before he is even tried?" (John 7:51 TLB).

This august group didn't listen to Nicodemus. In fact they did not answer his question; instead they simply diverted his logic by asking, "Are you from Galilee too?" (Are you defending him because you are His friend?) And then they stated, "Search the Scriptures and see for yourself—no prophets will ever come from Galilee!" (John 7:52 TLB).

Even though the Sanhedrin didn't listen to Nicodemus, he made an important point—and his willingness to stand up for Jesus showed that he had grown in his spiritual walk.

Later, after Jesus died on the cross, Nicodemus joined Joseph of Arimathea, asking Herod to allow them to bury the Lord. The man who had hidden in the shadows slowly came out into the light of day and professed his belief in his Savior. Jesus changed him forever.

And Jesus will also change your life—and the lives of those around you, through you. James Bryan Smith, Rich Mullins's biographer, wrote an article about how Mullins had changed his life, including his relationship with Jesus. Smith said, "Rich was absolutely dedicated to the person of Jesus Christ and fascinated by the whole concept of the incarnation. Sometimes I picture Jesus as a distant Savior, an alien God in a human suit who felt about as much as Mr. Spock. Rich showed me that Jesus was and is fully human, that He grew up just like me, that He felt what I feel, that He played with a dog who licked His nose and made angels in the winter snow, that Jesus laughed and cried and hurt just like me."[8]

Rich Mullins believed in Jesus so strongly that he sang about his belief over and over again. The lyrics of "I Believe" and "Creed" focus specifically on his strong faith in Christ. The words of "Creed" restate the Apostles' Creed, affirming Rich's belief in Jesus Christ as God's only begotten Son. Then he affirms:

> And I believe what I believe
> It's what makes me what I am,
> I did not make it, no it is making me.
> It is the very truth of God and not the invention of any man.[9]

These words are not only part of the chorus, which is repeated after every stanza, but Rich's belief in the doctrine of the Father, the Son, and the Holy Spirit echoes throughout the song. He states "I believe it" sixteen other times.

On September 17, 1997, Rich Mullins was killed in a horrible automobile accident on an Illinois road, but because of his belief he now lives forever with his Lord and Savior Jesus Christ.

Throughout his life he saw death as a part of life. "St. Francis is a big hero of mine," he said, "and Francis reminded himself daily that he would be dead. I think that while we live, the one sure thing about being alive is that we will die. Everything else is kind of 'iffy.' I mean, you may get rich, you may be poor. You may have a job tomorrow, you may not. Nothing is sure in life except that you will be dead.

"There's something really great about living in the awareness that we will someday die. For one thing, that makes all that is hard about life more endurable because we know it will pass, and it makes all that is good about life that much more valuable because it will pass. So I think that it teaches us to not hold on to things, to live with some sort of detachment. Not the sort of detachment where we are unmoved, but the sort of detachment where we allow ourselves to be moved easily and quickly, but we don't try to possess those things that move us."[10]

He believed, "Once you come to understand that life is unbelievably brief, and that we really can't do anything that's gonna change anything, that we don't really amount to a hill of beans—then all of a sudden you go, 'So it doesn't really matter if I'm not great. And if I don't have to be great, that means I can fail. And if I can fail, that means I can try. And if I can try, that means I'm gonna have a good time.'"[11]

Rich Mullins lived a pure life with the Lord, which is really freeing. Sometimes, when my life seems so complicated, I long for that myself. I know that the Lord's ways are not complicated or complex. They are really simple—and Rich lived that. He exemplified what Jesus wants us to be.

Rich's favorite song was "Elijah," a song he said was about his own death. In it, he said he would welcome the day he would leave earth for heaven.

After forty-one years of life, Rich Mullins crossed the Jordan. He is in heaven now, with his beloved Jesus. We who love Him and have received Him will all be there also someday.

FIFTEEN TRUTHS ABOUT JESUS
AND HIS RELATIONSHIP TO US

Look up the Scriptures that tell who Jesus is and write them in the spaces provided. Then express what this Scripture means to you in your daily life.

1. The Alpha and Omega (Revelation 21:6)

The significance of this verse to you:

2. The Bread of Life (John 6:35)

The significance of this verse to you:

3. The Chief Cornerstone (Ephesians 2:20)

The significance of this verse to you:

4. The Firstborn from the Dead (Colossians 1:18)

The significance of this verse to you:

5. **The Good Shepherd** (John 10:11)

The significance of this verse to you:

6. **The High Priest** (Hebrews 3:1)

The significance of this verse to you:

7. **Immanuel, "God with Us"** (Matthew 1:23)

The significance of this verse to you:

8. **The King of Kings and Lord of Lords** (Revelation 19:16)

The significance of this verse to you:

9. **The Chief Shepherd** (1 Peter 5:4)

The significance of this verse to you:

10. **The Lamb of God** (John 1:29)

The significance of this verse to you:

11. **The Light of the World** (John 9:5)

The significance of this verse to you:

12. **The Lord of Glory** (1 Corinthians 2:8)

The significance of this verse to you:

13. **The Mediator Between God and Men** (1 Timothy 2:5)

The significance of this verse to you:

14. The Prophet (Acts 3:22)

The significance of this verse to you:

15. The Savior (Luke 1:47)

The significance of this verse to you:

CHAPTER FOUR

Praying to Know God as Your Heavenly Father

A FRIEND OF MINE (WE'LL CALL HER ANN) WAS RAISED BY AN alcoholic father. Her mother was a strong woman who gave her support but was not vocal in her love, and her father was unable to give unconditional, steady love to her because of his addiction. More than that, she never felt she could trust him. He would go on binges, then promise to stop drinking. That never happened. For a few months he would seem to be normal, then the process would repeat itself. Over and over again he promised; over and over again he broke his promise to his daughter.

One Saturday afternoon when Ann was about ten she was playing at her house with two neighborhood boys. Her dad had left an empty bottle of beer sitting on a table beside the couch where the young boys sat.

One of the boys pointed to the bottle and said, "Your dad loves this more than he loves you."

Ann could not deny the statement, as much as it hurt her to hear what she inwardly knew—spoken by someone outside the family.

For a long time Ann had known she could not trust her dad, or count on him, or feel his love, but she refused to admit it, even to herself.

Later when Ann accepted Christ as Savior as an adult, she never prayed to

33

God as Father. She could address Him as Lord, but never as Father, as her friends did when they prayed aloud in Bible-study groups. And she had great difficulty trusting anyone, particularly God. Trust and faith were signs of true devotion to the Lord, she knew. But this knowledge was a part of her thinking, not something she felt in her heart. She never had the peace of truly believing the promise of Romans 8:28: "All things work together for good to those who love God, to those who are the called according to His purpose."

Often distortions of God's image come from our parental projections. I told of how this affected me in *Praying God's Will for Your Life*. I never had a dad who abused me, and for that I am very grateful. Yet my dad never rescued me from my abusive mother, and he was the only one with the power and authority to do so. Because of that experience, I subconsciously felt God would not help me either. I didn't openly rebel against or resent God; instead I just felt forgotten.

Just as I projected my dad's parenting onto my image of God, many children who have been abused often do so. In fact, all of us derive part of our image of God from our parents. We project these pictures onto God as a movie projector projects an actor's picture onto a movie screen. And counselors say that most people see God through the lens of their fathers, who is, like God, the authority figure in the home.

Are you like my friend Ann? Has your image of God been distorted by a distant, addicted, or abusive parent? Examine your relationship with the heavenly Father and check any of the following statements that apply to you:

_____ I doubt that I am a beloved son or daughter to my heavenly Father.

_____ I feel distant from Him.

_____ I am angry with Him.

_____ I feel abandoned by Him.

_____ I never feel I can trust Him.

_____ The thought of my heavenly Father brings tears of pain rather than feelings of joy.

If any one of these statements applies to you, you need a greater understanding of your heavenly Father's love for you.

Read through the following Scriptures and insert your name in the blank spaces:

> Yet in all these things we are more than conquerors through Him who loved us. For I, _____, am persuaded that neither death nor life, nor angels nor principalities nor powers, nor things present nor things to come, nor height, nor depth, nor any other created thing, shall be able to separate us from the love of God which is in Christ Jesus our Lord. (Romans 8:37–39)

> "I will be a Father to you, _____,
> And you shall be My sons and daughters,"
> Says the LORD Almighty. (2 Corinthians 6:18)

The almighty God of the universe is calling out to you as a father does to his beloved child. This is the moment to take inventory of your image of God so you can answer His call.

DIMENSIONS OF OUR IMAGE OF GOD

Dr. Larry Stephens identified four different dimensions of our image of God in his book, *Please Let Me Know You, God*. These dimensions were discovered as Dr. Stephens, a licensed professional counselor, met with patients over many years. The four dimensions are:

- the intellectual dimension (the layer of our conscious beliefs),
- the symbolic dimension (when we associate God with certain word pictures, like the good shepherd and the lamb who was slain for us),
- the spiritual dimension (the degree to which we experience God from His Spirit living within us), and
- the emotional dimension (our feelings toward God, which are expressed in the list above).

The more these dimensions agree with one another, the less distortion there is in our image of God. The less they agree, the more distortion we experience.[1]

Check the statements that apply to you below to assess the extent of your distortion in these areas:

The Intellectual Dimension
- God loves me.
- God is loving.
- God is not available.

The Symbolic Dimension
- God is light. God is love. God is my loving Father.
- God is a protector, a king, a judge.
- God is invisible or nonexistent. God is my enemy.

The Spiritual Dimension
- I am secure in God.
- I am uncertain.
- I am alone and empty.

The Emotional Dimension
- I feel loved, accepted, forgiven, and joyful.
- I feel confused, anxious, and abandoned.
- I feel angry or lonely. I am in despair.

You may have already realized that the first statement in each list is the most biblically accurate. If you checked these first statements, or checked them in three out of the four dimensions, you have a healthy image of God. If you checked the second statements in most of these categories, your image of God is distorted. If you checked the third statements, your image of God is severely distorted.[2]

We can all make the choice to either change our image of God or remain locked in our present understanding of Him. To begin this process read through the following list of descriptions of God in the Bible, which were penned by people who knew Him well (for a longer list, look at pages 40–43 at the end of this chapter).

First, statements from King David in the Old Testament:

I will sing of the mercies of the LORD forever;
With my mouth will I make known
Your faithfulness to all generations. (Psalm 89:1)

God is our refuge and strength, a very present help in trouble. (Psalm 46:1)

Second, statements from the apostle Paul in the New Testament:

> But God, who is rich in mercy, because of His great love with which He loved us, even when we were dead in trespasses, made us alive together with Christ (by grace you have been saved), and raised us up together, and made us sit together in the heavenly places in Christ Jesus. (Ephesians 2:4–7)

Some of you may see the God you imagined here. If not, do you accept the testimony of these men in the Bible as true? If so, this God is also your heavenly Father, One who loves you, who is faithful to you, who is your refuge and strength. It's your choice to accept Him as who He is.

If you are willing to do this, say the prayer below:

> God, I acknowledge You as my heavenly Father today. Heal any misconception I have of You. Where my earthly father has failed me and I have blamed You, forgive me and take away that hurt. I long to receive the inheritance that You have promised Your children.

Once you have done this, you need to be reparented by God. In his book, Dr. Larry Stephens suggests a four-step process that has benefited his patients.

REPARENTED BY GOD

Step One: Make a conscious decision to separate any negative experiences in your past—particularly experiences with your parents—from your image of God.

In the past you have confused the image of God by projecting onto Him your parents' traits. From now on, choose to replace this distorted image of God with the truth of who God is. To do so, go through the list of God's attributes on pages 40–43. Write in the Scripture verses and as you write them, see God in the images portrayed there. Then copy the Scriptures that are most significant to you onto index cards to carry in your purse or place wherever they can be conveniently read throughout the day.

Step Two: Make a conscious decision to start over with God.

God has given each of us a clean slate. He says, "Though your sins are like scarlet, they shall be as white as snow. Though they are red like crimson, they shall be as wool" (Isaiah 1:18). Are you willing to give Him a new opportunity to walk with you as your friend, helper, and Father from this day on?

Remember to accept God for who He is—your heavenly Father, your *abba* (which in Aramaic means "daddy"). In Romans the apostle Paul tells the early Christians, "For as many as are led by the Spirit of God, these are sons of God. For you did not receive the spirit of bondage again to fear, but you received the Spirit of adoption by whom we cry out, 'Abba, Father'" (8:14–15).

Jesus was the first person to call God by this name. When He was praying in the Garden of Gethsemane, He cried out, "Abba, Father, all things are possible for You. Take this cup away from Me; nevertheless, not what I will, but what You will" (Mark 14:36).

In Jesus' time the Jews did not even say the name of God, and even today they write His name as G—D. Yet Christians have been given the right to call this same God, "Daddy." He is a parent who loves you, a Father whom you can trust. He promises in Scripture, "I will not leave you orphans; I will come to you" (John 14:18).

Step Three: In prayer, invite God to be your Father of choice.

Many children who have distant dads, addicted dads, or abusive dads reach out as children to God as their Father. My friend Ann certainly did. She prayed to Him as a child to be with her and protect her. She even consciously thought, *I might not have a dad here on earth, but I do have a Father in heaven.* As an adult, however, this childish faith (like a lot of other genuine childish beliefs) became shadowy and indistinct. When she left her childhood home and began raising her own children, problems of finances and parenting overwhelmed her. She and others like her need to reaffirm their desire to know God as heavenly Father.

If you wish to do so, say the following prayer:

Dear heavenly Father,

I know that You love me. I know that You are there for me. I desire to know You fully as my heavenly Father, my *abba*. Help me to see You in the Scriptures as You really are, and then to make that image a part of my life.

Step Four: As you approach your heavenly Father, come as a child.[3]

One day when some parents brought their children to Jesus to have Him bless them, Jesus told the disciples who were trying to keep the children away, "Let the little children come to me, and do not forbid them, for the kingdom of God belongs to such as these. I tell you the truth," He said, "anyone who will not receive the kingdom of God like a little child will never enter it" (Luke 18:15 NIV). Jesus was telling them—and us—that we need to have childlike attitudes of acceptance, faith, and trust, all the attitudes that my friend Ann had as a child and lost as she grew up.

Ann and others like her need to think back to their childhoods and remember the faith and love they had for God. Then they need to hold on to these feelings as they look to the future.

As Ann progressed through her life, she was able to renew her childlike faith. Part of what helped her to do so was seeing God's hand throughout her struggles. She could think to herself, *God helped me through this; He will help me now as I work through other problems.*

And He did.

FIFTEEN ATTRIBUTES OF GOD

Look up the Scriptures that testify to each particular attribute of God and write them in the spaces below each attribute. As you do so, see God in that picture and write what this Scripture means to you in your daily life. Finally write the Scriptures that are most significant to you on an index card that you can carry in your purse or place on your vanity mirror.

1. He is my Redeemer (Isaiah 59:20).

The significance of this verse to you:

2. He is my Patience (Romans 15:5).

The significance of this verse to you:

3. He is my Truth (John 14:6).

The significance of this verse to you:

4. He is my Overcomer (John 16:33).

The significance of this verse to you:

5. **He is my Light (John 8:12).**

The significance of this verse to you:

6. **He is the Power of God (1 Corinthians 1:24).**

The significance of this verse to you:

7. **He is my Bread of Life (John 6:35).**

The significance of this verse to you:

8. **He is the Author of my faith (Hebrews 12:2).**

The significance of this verse to you:

9. He is my Peace (Ephesians 2:14).

The significance of this verse to you:

10. He is my Rewarder (Hebrews 11:6).

The significance of this verse to you:

11. He is my Wisdom of God (1 Corinthians 1:24).

The significance of this verse to you:

12. He is my Purifier (Malachi 3:3).

The significance of this verse to you:

13. He is my Refiner (Malachi 3:2–3).

The significance of this verse to you:

14. He is my Resurrection (John 11:25).

The significance of this verse to you:

15. He is the Lifter of my head (Psalm 3:3).

The significance of this verse to you:

CHAPTER FIVE

Praying to Know God as the Holy Spirit

MAX ANDERS, WHO IS AN AUTHOR AND FORMER PASTOR, ADMITS that as a college student he lived a foolish and sinful lifestyle. He played cards in the student union all day instead of attending classes and played drums in a rock band all night. He also adopted some of the lifestyles of those around him at college where drinking, drugs, vulgar language, sexual freedom, cheating, and stealing were cherished values. All of this brought him to such despair that he was ready to listen when Jake Berger told him about Jesus very late on the night of September 1, 1966.

At that moment Max's greatest concern was trying to become a Christian and then not being able to pull it off. He said, "Jake, I've turned over new leaves before, and they never stayed turned over."

"Becoming a Christian isn't like turning over a new leaf," Jake replied. "When you invite Christ into your life, you are born again. The Holy Spirit comes into your life and will help you live the new life Christ calls you to."

For some reason, Max assumed that he ought to *feel* this happen. In his mind he imagined a Max-shaped Spirit sitting beside him, and as he prayed for Christ to save him and for the Holy Spirit to come into his life, he actually felt something. But he seemed to lose that feeling after a while.[1]

Max now knows that "the concept of indwelling is such a mystery that probably none of us understands specifically what happens in the process. But indwelt we are if we give our lives over to following Christ."[2]

He has also learned that the guilt he felt was the convicting ministry of the Holy Spirit. "The deep remorse, the sense of meaninglessness, the longing for something better were all part of His ministry in bringing me to salvation . . .

"This is the reason it is so important for Christians or non-Christians to respond whenever they feel drawn to God and away from sin . . . A person must have the ministry of the Holy Spirit to become a Christian."[3]

How about you? If you think you don't need the Holy Spirit in your life, ask yourself the questions below:

1. Would you like to feel God's love for you? _____ yes _____ no

2. Do you need help living according to God's Word and in making wise, right choices? _____ yes _____ no

3. Would you like prayer support from on high? _____ yes _____ no

4. Would you like a teacher to help you understand God's Word in the Bible and Christ's teachings? _____ yes _____ no

5. Would you like insight into future events? _____ yes _____ no

If you answered yes to the above questions, you are looking for the power of the Holy Spirit in your life, because He functions as a part of the Godhead to give all Christians this help.

THE WORK OF THE HOLY SPIRIT

Let's look at 5 ways the Holy Spirit works within us:

1. To Reaffirm God's Love for Us

In Paul's letters to the churches he is trying to help other Christians grow spiritually as many good mentors do today. He knows what has been essential in his relationship with the Father, and he wants others to experience that same blessing. Without doubt the Holy Spirit's ministry has been important to Paul in his everyday life. Some theologians believe that the book of Romans is the most significant of Paul's epistles. Paul first introduces the ministry of the Holy Spirit in this epistle in chapter 5. He says, "Now hope does not disappoint, because the love of God has been poured out in our hearts by the Holy Spirit who was given to us" (5:5). When we feel God's love at a church service or from the love of a family member or friend, the Holy Spirit confirms that feeling within us. And He also reminds us of God's love through the fact that Christ died for us when we were weak and unable to overcome our sins (v. 6). The Holy Spirit also gives us the power to do what is right.

2. To Give Us the Power to Do What Is Right

Paul struggled with the same temptations that we do every day. In Romans 7:15 he confesses, "For what I will to do, that I do not practice; but what I hate, that I do." He concludes the chapter by saying, "With the mind I myself serve the law of God, but with the flesh the law of sin" (v. 25). Like us, Paul cannot fully overcome the temptation to sin. And let's be clear about this. Paul is not talking about the man in the local jail, his neighbors, his spouses, or his children. Paul is talking about himself—and us. We are all tempted to sin.

In his commentary *Thru the Bible*, J. Vernon McGee says, "The truth is that man is the enemy of God . . . Man in his natural condition, if taken to heaven, would start a revolution, and he would have a protest meeting going on before the sun went down."[4] Sounds more like Screwtape and Wormwood and their boss, the devil, than a child of God. But that's the description of human beings without the work of the Holy Spirit.

All of us need the Holy Spirit, who works for our sanctification, the process that enables us to resist sin and become more like Christ. The Holy Spirit is mentioned nineteen times in Romans 8 as Paul searches for an answer to his dilemma of wanting to do what is right, but succumbing to doing wrong. Paul warned the Roman Christians: "For if you live according to the flesh you will die; but if by the Spirit you put to death the deeds of the body, you will live. For as many as are led by the Spirit of God, these are sons of God" (Romans 8:13–14).

Paul gave this same warning to the Galatian Christians: "I say then: Walk in the Spirit, and you shall not fulfill the lust of the flesh. For the flesh lusts against the Spirit, and the Spirit against the flesh; and these are contrary to one another, so that you do not do the things that you wish" (Galatians 5:16–17).

And so that we can be clear about sin, Paul enumerates the sins of the flesh in the next verses—adultery, hatred, jealousies, selfish ambitions, envy, drunkenness, and the like.

The New Living Translation renders some of the sins in Galatians a little differently, bringing them even closer to home: quarreling, outbursts of anger, the feeling that everyone is wrong except those in your own little group, and wild parties.

Then Paul goes on to mention the fruits of the Spirit, the signs that the Holy Spirit lives within a person: love, joy, peace, longsuffering, kindness, goodness, faithfulness, gentleness, and self-control.

Now I ask you, How would you like to live? In selfish ambition, envy, drunkenness, and outbursts of anger? Or in love, joy, and peace?

If the apostle Paul needed the Holy Spirit to win the war against sin within himself, certainly we all need this Helper.

The Holy Spirit also prays for us.

3. To Pray for Us

Do you sometimes feel as if you don't know what to pray? God has sent the Holy Spirit to help us when we don't know what words to say. Paul tells the Roman Christians, "Likewise the Spirit also helps in our weaknesses. For we do not know what we should pray for as we ought, but the Spirit Himself makes intercession for us with groanings which cannot be uttered. Now He who searches the hearts knows what the mind of the Spirit is, because He makes intercession for the saints according to the will of God" (Romans 8:26–27).

Sometimes I am relieved when I can pray, "Lord, I don't know what to ask for in this situation of _____, but I want Your will to be done." Then I trust the Holy Spirit to intercede for me or this person according to God's will.

The Holy Spirit reaffirms God's love for us, gives us the power to do what is right, prays for us, and also teaches us the words of Christ.

4. To Teach Us the Words of Christ

The disciples had many questions for Jesus as He prepared them for His coming death at the Last Supper. Thomas said, "Lord, we do not know where You are going, and how can we know the way?" (John 14:5). Philip said, "Lord, show us the Father, and it is sufficient for us" (v. 8). Knowing that He was leaving them,

47

they panicked and tried to reconcile all they had been taught into some kind of theology that would keep them in the days ahead.

Jesus knew they would need more than that. Physically He was departing, but the Spirit could continue to be present with them. He promised His bewildered followers that "the Helper, the Holy Spirit, whom the Father will send in My name, He will teach you all things, and bring to your remembrance all things that I said to you" (John 14:26).

If the disciples who sat at Jesus' feet needed the Holy Spirit to help them grow in their understanding of His words, how much more do we also need this guidance?

5. To Give Us Insight into Future Events

At the Last Supper, Jesus went on to assure the disciples that the Holy Spirit would give them insight into the future without Him. "When He, the Spirit of truth, has come, He will guide you into all truth; for He will not speak on His own authority, but whatever He hears He will speak; and *He will tell you things to come*" (John 16:13, emphasis added).

If you have accepted Christ as your Savior, you have also received the Holy Spirit. Hear Jesus saying the following words to you, just as He said them to His disciples. (Write your name in the blank spaces below.)

> And I will pray the Father, and He will give you, _____, another Helper, that He may abide with you forever—the Spirit of truth, whom the world cannot receive, because it neither sees Him nor knows Him; but you, _____, know Him, for He dwells with you and will be in you, _____.

Now look for the Holy Spirit's ministry in your life. He will lead and guide you as you encounter problems and make decisions.

HOW DOES THE HOLY SPIRIT LEAD AND GUIDE US?

Max Anders, a pastor who has written several books to help laymen understand the Bible and biblical truths, mentions four ways the Holy Spirit leads and guides us in his book, *What You Need to Know about the Holy Spirit*.

He says that the Holy Spirit leads us providentially, through Scripture, through the counsel of others, and through inclinations, thoughts, or desires in our hearts.

Providentially. If circumstances prohibit us from doing something, this may well be the will of God for us.

Through Scripture. After I accepted Christ as Savior, I was able to understand the Bible and to hear God's message to me as never before. I received this insight through the Holy Spirit within me.

Through the counsel of others. Proverbs teaches that there is safety in a multitude of counselors: "Where there is no counsel, the people fall; but in the multitude of counselors there is safety" (11:14). Pastors, Christian counselors, and enlightened laypersons can give us direction from the insight of the Holy Spirit within them.

Through the inclinations, thoughts, or desires in our minds. God plants inclinations, thoughts, or desires in our minds to lead and guide us. Max Anders warns that this can be dangerous because "it is often difficult to know whether something in our head is our own personal desire or perhaps even a deception by the evil one."[5]

In this case, he recommends that we retrace the above principles. First, do circumstances tell us anything? In other words, have we been blocked from doing this before? If so, maybe it is not God's will for us. Second, does Scripture tell us anything? Would doing this violate either the commandments of God or the teachings of Jesus? Third, is there an agreement from an abundance of godly wisdom? Have we sought the advice of several Christians whom we trust? Finally, if we have followed these steps and we still don't sense any direct leading or guiding from the Lord, Anders says we are free to do as we please. He quotes the great Reformer Martin Luther, who said, "Love God and do as you please."

This seems to contradict God's call for obedience to certain biblical principles, but Luther meant, "If you love God, you will automatically obey His commandments."[6]

Several years ago Christians began wearing wristbands with the initials WWJD written on them in white. This was to remind them to ask the question "What would Jesus do?" when they were confronted with a problem or a decision. These people were automatically testing their circumstances against God's Word in the Bible. They wanted to obey His commandments because they loved Him. No coercion was needed. Just the love of their heavenly Father—and the guidance of the Holy Spirit.

Stop now and write a prayer, asking God to help you understand all you need to know about the Holy Spirit's working in your life. Ask Him to fill you with the Holy Spirit in a fresh new way this day—and in the future.

THE HOLY SPIRIT'S ROLES

Several passages of Scripture show the role of the Holy Spirit. Write the passages in the space below the Scripture notations and then note how you see the Holy Spirit functioning in this instance.

Genesis 1:2

I see the Holy Spirit functioning in this passage as:

Psalm 139:7

I see the Holy Spirit functioning in this passage as:

Acts 5:1–4

I see the Holy Spirit functioning in this passage as:

1 Corinthians 2:9–10

I see the Holy Spirit functioning in this passage as:

1 Corinthians 12:4–11

I see the Holy Spirit functioning in this passage as:

Ephesians 4:30–32

I see the Holy Spirit functioning in this passage as:

If you would like to learn more about the Holy Spirit, I recommend that you read Max Anders's book *The Holy Spirit: Knowing Our Comforter.*

THE HOLY SPIRIT THROUGHOUT THE BIBLE

Sometimes we tend to think of the Holy Spirit as only functioning in Jesus' time. But the Holy Spirit is active throughout Scripture. Some of those instances are listed below. Read the passages and write the verses below the notation. If a whole chapter of Scripture is indicated, only write the verses that particularly speak to you.

Judges 15:14–15

2 Samuel 23:1–2

Matthew 4:1–11

Luke 1:35

Luke 4:18

Acts 2

Acts 9:10–19

Acts 10:38

Romans 1:4

CHAPTER SIX

Praying to Know God as Lord over Every Area of Your Life

WE WERE SO POOR WHEN I WAS A CHILD THAT I WAS EMBARRASSED to invite friends to my home. Our house was a shack in the middle of a weed-filled lot. Sometimes rats crawled across my bed at night.

When I grew up and left home, I always worked very hard so I could afford a decent place to live. That kind of security became very important to me because I never wanted to return to the conditions of my childhood. I feared that if I were to really surrender my life to the Lord, He might require that of me.

Once I accepted God as Savior, as Father, and as Holy Spirit, I realized I needed to expose many areas of my life to the Lord's control. This was difficult for me because it called for deepening trust. Until then I'd had few positive experiences when someone other than myself was in control of my life.

The threat that God will ask more of us than we are willing to give is the reason, I believe, some of us are unwilling to go deeper in our faith. God might ask us to live in conditions with which we would not feel comfortable—a meager home, less income, an old car—or even require us to become missionaries and give up everything. I now know that He's not going to ask all of us to do those things, but He does want to know that we would be willing to say yes if He did. He wants to know if we will love Him with all our hearts, with all our souls, and with all our minds and surrender everything to Him.

In every house I lived in when I was growing up, we had rooms that no one was allowed to see. They contained a confusing clutter of items rendered useless by their overwhelming number and lack of order. One reason my mother never wanted anyone to come to our house (aside from the fact that it was too exhausting for her to keep up a front of normalcy) was that she was afraid someone would see the secret rooms, which were reflective of our family life. Once I grew up, it was as if those secret rooms in our home became secret places in my heart. I kept so many parts of me hidden that I lived in terror that they would be discovered and I'd be rejected.

When I first received Jesus into my heart, I showed Him into the guest room. The problem was, He wasn't content to stay there. He kept knocking on one door after another until I was opening doors to rooms I had never known were there.

GIVING HIM THE RUN OF THE HOUSE

When you invite Jesus into the home of your being (by being born again), you are supposed to also give Him the "run of the house" (by making Him Lord over your life). However, many of us are slow to do that completely.

Are you afraid of what God will ask of you? Take an inventory of the rooms in your own house. Check the areas below that you have not opened to the Lord:

_____ My finances

_____ My job

_____ My home

_____ My possessions

_____ My future

_____ My relationship with my mom or dad

_____ My relationship with my boyfriend

_____ My relationship with my husband

_____ My relationship with my children

_____ My relationship with my boss

_____ My relationship with my fellow workers

_____ My relationship with my friends and acquaintances

_____ My past

If you checked any of the above, ask yourself why you are not willing to allow Jesus into these areas of your life. Write each area below and then give the answer:

Do you hesitate to believe that God can be trusted with every area of your life? If so, read the Scripture below as though Jesus were speaking to you directly, inserting your name in the blank space I have added to the verses:

> Trust in the LORD with all your heart, _____,
> And lean not on your own understanding;
> In all your ways acknowledge Him,
> And He shall direct your paths. (Proverbs 3:5–6)

Notice that word *all*. It's very specific. If we want things to work out well, we have to acknowledge Him as Lord over *all* areas of our lives. I had to be willing to give God the right-of-way by frequently saying, "Jesus, be Lord over every area of my life." Then as He pointed to places where I had not opened the door to Him, I let Him in.

I found out that when He knocks on different doors inside us, He will never bulldoze His way in and break down the walls. He will simply knock persistently and quietly and, as He's invited, will come to gently occupy each corner of our lives to clean and rebuild.

I am very aware that each of us who has a house that is warm and dry is very fortunate when others are living in shacks. Because I am thankful, I have asked the Lord to be Lord over all of my material blessings. If He's in charge of them, and I'm willing to let go of them—to live somewhere else or give away what I have—then it is possible to be sensitive to the Spirit, and I want to be sensitive to His Spirit. I want Him to be in charge of whatever I have so I don't cling to *it* rather than to *Him*. I want to hold what I have with open arms so that He can move through it and use it for His glory.

I know that God doesn't want us to feel guilty when He gives us blessings. Still He doesn't want us to live a lavish lifestyle either. If I want to acquire something, I say, "Is this alright with You, Lord? Because if You don't want me to have it, I don't want it."

Every so often we need to restate this principle to ourselves. We need to say, "Lord, I put You as Lord over my marriage today. I ask You to be Lord over my finances. Be Lord over my eating habits and care for my body. Be Lord over my relationships."

Or "Lord, I give You this child. I establish You as Ruler over this parent/child relationship." Or "Lord, this is what I'd like to buy. If You want me to do something else with this money—if this should go to missions or the poor, open my heart to it. Speak to me, Holy Spirit, and I'll do it."

Acknowledging God as Lord over every area of your life is an ongoing act of will. Because of that I recommend that you write a prayer below, asking Him to be Lord over every area of your life and asking for His help to walk in His perfect will in all that you do and everything you say. Then repeat this prayer every morning when you wake up.

SCRIPTURE TO ENCOURAGE
YOU TO OPEN EVERY AREA OF YOUR LIFE

As you begin to open the rooms of your heart, read the first two Scriptures and write them in the spaces so you can remember how God sees this process.

1 Peter 2:4–5

Psalm 51:17

Now work through these Scriptures of encouragement, writing them in the spaces below the passages. If one is particularly meaningful to you, copy it onto an index card so you can reread it as you give Jesus the run of the house.

2 Peter 1:9–10

Hebrews 10:35–39

1 Peter 2:4–5

Isaiah 42:16

CHAPTER SEVEN

Praying to Know God as a Name That Answers Your Every Need

LIKE ANY HIGH SCHOOL SENIOR, JENNIFER RUNDLE LOOKED FORWARD to graduation activities at her Virginia Beach school. A popular teenager, she wanted to celebrate this milestone in her life with her friends—by joining them at prom, graduation parties, and summer days at the beach. But she was missing out on a lot. The sharp pain in her abdomen, which had begun five years earlier, was crippling on some days. She had been going to doctors for the problem, but the only definite diagnosis had been anemia, which had been treated. Though she felt worse and worse, she wanted to have fun. These were her last days to be with her high school friends.

Then Jennifer and her mom noticed a lump on her side that seemed to come and go. Her mom called her aunt, who was a doctor, and she advised them to see a gastroenterologist who quickly ordered a new round of tests at a local hospital.

This time the diagnosis was clear: Jennifer had a malignant tumor growing in her colon—almost unheard of in someone her age. Surgery would be scheduled immediately.

"Surgery?" Jen asked her parents and the doctor. "I won't need surgery," she said. "Jesus will heal me."

Jennifer was admitted to the hospital and prayed fervently to keep up her faith. She knew God could heal her, and she and her parents prayed daily for a healing. Her dad helped her search the Bible for God's promises about healing and protection, and she taped them to her hospital-room wall, one above the other, so the doctors and nurses and every visitor who entered the room could not help but comment on the unusual wallpaper.

Still, the days went by, and Jennifer's condition remained unchanged. Surgery loomed ever closer. *Why*, Jen wondered, *is God taking so long with my miracle?*

Millions of other people have asked the same question. Certainly I did. Before I came to know the Lord, I had recurring nightmares. When I told a good friend about these frightening dreams, she advised, "When that happens, just speak the name of Jesus over and over. It will take the fear away."

"That's it?" I replied, doubtful yet willing to do anything she said if it would help.

The next time I woke out of a nightmare, I immediately remembered Terry's advice.

"Jesus," I whispered as I gasped for air. "Jesus!" I called louder and held my breath for a moment. "Jesus, Jesus, Jesus," I said again and again as though clinging for life to the sound of that word. In a few minutes the fear lifted.

That was my first experience with the power of Jesus' name, and I have never forgotten it. I didn't even know Him at the time, yet when I called Him, He gave me peace and freedom from fear.

A NAME FOR ALL SEASONS

Certain guarantees and rewards are inherent in simply acknowledging the name of Jesus. The Lord has many names in the Bible, and each one expresses an aspect of His nature or one of His attributes. When we acknowledge Him by those names, we invite Him to be those things to us. For example, He is called Healer. When we pray, "Jesus, You are my Healer," and mix it with faith, it brings this attribute to bear upon our lives. Jesus is my Healer. Jesus is your Healer. Jesus was also Jennifer Rundle's healer.

Unfortunately we will all suffer at different times in our lives. Such suffering can occur in three different ways:

1. Physical Suffering

Jennifer was suffering from the malignant tumor in her colon. Other people may suffer because they are injured. In the Bible, a nurse dropped Jonathan's son, Mephibosheth, as she carried him away from Jerusalem after Jonathan was killed in battle. She knew there would be major controversy over who would be the next king, and she didn't want the child killed in the skirmishes. This injury caused Mephibosheth to be lame for the rest of his life. Like him, a person could be permanently injured. Or someone could have a recurrent pain from a bad back. Or suffer from heart disease.

Do you have some physical pain or disease? If so, you are not alone. God will walk with you.

2. Mental Suffering

All of us experience some distress, some worry or apprehension or depression. The apostle Paul spoke of such suffering. In his first letter to the Corinthians he said he didn't come with excellence of speech or wisdom, but "in weakness, in fear, and in much trembling" (2:3). In his second letter to them he said, "For we do not want you to be ignorant, brethren, of our trouble which came to us in Asia: that we were burdened beyond measure, above strength, so that we despaired even of life" (1:8). And then in the seventh chapter of this second letter, he said, "For indeed, when we came to Macedonia, our flesh had no rest but we were troubled on every side. Outside were conflicts, inside were fears" (v. 5).

If the apostle Paul was beset by these emotional downturns, we cannot expect our lives to be free from them.

Are you suffering as Paul was? If so, explain how in the space below.

3. Spiritual Suffering

This suffering can come from the world, the flesh, or the devil. Such suffering is real, and again, the apostle Paul experienced it (Romans 7:18–24). We will talk more about this in Chapter 16.

Many people ask, "Why does a loving and wise God permit His children to suffer?" Certainly Jennifer Rundle had a reason to ask this question; her chances of getting colon cancer as a teenager were minuscule.

Are you suffering spiritually? Are some questions about God and His relationship to you lingering in your mind? If so, write them in the space below:

The Scriptures offer a number of reasons for suffering; the ones that I will mention here are taken from Thomas Nelson's *The New Open Bible*.

PURPOSES FOR SUFFERING

Scripture gives seven purposes for suffering, which help us endure these difficult times.[1]

1. To Glorify God

Twice Jesus said that people—a blind man and Lazarus—suffered so that God would be glorified. In John 9:1–3 His disciples ask Him, "Rabbi, who sinned, this man or his parents, that he was born blind?" And Jesus answers, "Neither this man nor his parents sinned, but that the works of God should be revealed in him." And in chapter 11, Jesus tells Martha and Mary that their brother's sickness "is not unto death, but for the glory of God, that the Son of God may be glorified through it" (vv. 1–4).

Jennifer Rundle found this to be true in her life. Three days before her surgery, Jennifer was sitting on her hospital bed, praying with her parents.

"What's wrong with what we're praying?" Jen asked her parents. "What's wrong with our faith? Why have I not been healed?"

"I don't know," her dad admitted.

So they decided to change the focus of their prayers. Instead of asking God to heal Jennifer, they asked, "What do You want to do, Lord?"

That was a revolutionary step for Jennifer. As they prayed for God's guidance in her situation, the words from Ephesians 3:20, a verse she had memorized in Bible study, consumed her heart and mind: "Now to him who is able to do immeasurably more than all we ask or imagine, according to his power that is at work within us, to him be glory in the church and in Christ Jesus throughout all generations" (NIV). It was as if God was speaking to her directly.

She opened her eyes and told her parents. "I know what the Lord wants to do," she said. "The Lord just said two things. First, He wants to do more than we are asking or imagining. And second, He wants us to pray that He will be glorified."

Suddenly Jennifer became grateful for her circumstances. No longer would she put God in a box; God was about to do something important through this—even if it meant she had to have an operation.

Word of Jen's condition spread. People in the hospital began asking Jennifer and her family about their faith. Doctors, nurses, and patients all heard the gospel, and many accepted Christ. The local newspaper picked up her story and ran an article, complete with photographs of Jennifer and her patchwork wallpaper. Four follow-up pieces later, Jen found herself deluged with visitors, calls, and letters—many from people she had never met.

One card in particular caught Jennifer's attention. It was from a woman who, reeling from desperate financial circumstances after a bitter divorce, had decided to kill herself. Contemplating her choice on the morning she had decided to commit suicide, the woman had poured herself a cup of coffee and stared, distractedly, at the morning paper. She saw Jennifer's picture and read the article. As the words sank into her mind her outlook began to change. "If this teenager can find joy in Jesus," she resolved, "then so can I."[2]

Can you think of a time when your suffering gave glory to the Lord? Describe that experience below and how the Lord was glorified through it:

2. To Produce Fruit

If we allow suffering to accomplish its purpose, it can bring forth patience (Hebrews 10:36; James 1:3), joy (Psalms 30:5; 126:6), knowledge (Psalm 94:12), and maturity (1 Peter 5:10).

Can you think of a difficult time that has benefited you, making you more patient or more mature or giving you more knowledge of yourself or your surroundings? Describe the experience and how you benefited at the top of the next page:

3. To Make Us Like Jesus

We become more like Jesus as we deal positively with our suffering. The apostle Paul testified to this truth in his own life. He said that his persecution was "that I may know Him and the power of His resurrection, and the fellowship of His sufferings, being conformed to His death" (Philippians 3:10).

Has the suffering you experienced made you become more like our model, the Lord Jesus Christ? Note how this happened below:

4. To Teach Us Dependence

The apostle Paul also talked about a "thorn in the flesh," a pain that continually troubled him. He said, "I pleaded with the Lord three times that it might depart from me. And He said to me, 'My grace is sufficient for you, for My strength is made perfect in weakness.' Therefore most gladly I will rather boast in my infirmities, that the power of Christ may rest upon me. Therefore I take pleasure in infirmities, in reproaches, in needs, in persecutions, in distresses, for Christ's sake. For when I am weak, then I am strong" (2 Corinthians 12:1–10).

Has your suffering made it obvious to you that neither you nor anyone else can completely ease the pain? Has it become quite evident that you must rely on the Lord for help in this difficult time?

Suffering can glorify God, produce fruit in our lives (patience, joy, knowledge, and maturity), make us like Jesus, teach us dependence upon God, and refine our lives.

5. To Refine Our Lives

Psalm 66 is a song of praise to God for all He has done. Yet the psalm clearly states that the writer has experienced suffering:

> For You, O God, have proved us;
> You have refined us as silver is refined.
> You brought us into the net;
> You laid affliction on our backs.
> You have caused men to ride over our heads:
> We went through fire and through water;
> But You brought us out to rich fulfillment. (vv. 10–12)

The psalm was written after the author had been involved in a great battle, one where the outcome seemed grim. Yet when the writer cried out to the Lord, God heard him. "He has attended to the voice of my prayer," the author says. "Blessed be God, who has not turned away my prayer, nor His mercy from me!" (Psalm 66:19–20).

Could God be refining your life during one of these difficult times? If so, how?

6. To Rebuke Our Sin

As a faithful earthly father punishes his erring child, so does our heavenly Father. The writer of Hebrews makes this very clear to the early Jewish believers in Hebrews 12:5–9. He first reminds them what God has said to them previously:

> My son, do not despise the chastening of the LORD,
> Nor be discouraged when you are rebuked by Him,
> For whom the LORD loves He chastens,
> And scourges every son whom He receives.

Then the writer goes on to say, "If you endure chastening, God deals with you as with sons; for what son is there whom a father does not chasten? But if you are without chastening, of which all have become partakers, then you are illegitimate and not sons . . ." (vv. 7–8).

Personally, I'd rather endure God's loving punishment as His child than be in the camp of those who are not truly His—the illegitimate.

Finally the writer consoles his readers by telling them the end of the story of their suffering: "Now no chastening seems to be joyful for the present, but grievous; nevertheless, afterward it yields the peaceable fruit of righteousness to those who have been trained by it" (v. 11). And the writer encourages them to endure until the end is reached: "Therefore strengthen the hands which hang down, and the feeble knees, and make straight paths for your feet, so that what is lame may not be dislocated, but rather be healed" (v. 12).

My feelings are similar to the writer of Psalm 66. My hands have hung down limply at my side because I have been discouraged, and my knees have seemed feeble, but I am willing to persevere when I know that healing is at the end of my journey.

How about you? Could God be chastening you for something you have done? If so, accept His punishment as just and look forward to the healing that He promises.

7. To Enlarge Our Ministry toward Others

In the opening to Paul's second letter to the Corinthians he says, "Blessed be the God and Father of our Lord Jesus Christ, the Father of mercies and God of all comfort, who comforts us in all our tribulation, that we may be able to comfort those who are in any trouble, with the comfort with which we ourselves are comforted by God" (1:3–4).

I know a man who suffered a heart attack. When he was in the hospital, another man who had recovered from a heart attack visited with him, sharing his own struggles with heart disease. No one could have encouraged this patient more than someone who had "walked the walk" before him. In the same way, if a woman has had difficulty in her marriage and worked through these problems successfully, she is the best supporter of another woman who is going through the same difficulties.

Do you suppose that God would like to use your past suffering to bless someone else? Do you know someone who is struggling with the same difficulty now? If so, ask the Lord if He would have you reach out to this person. It could be that He wants you to enlarge your ministry to others.

Stop for a moment and write a prayer, asking God to help you understand the suffering you are experiencing—and to use it for His glory:

You can be sure that God will walk with you through difficult times. If you ask for His help, He will fight for you.

GOD'S ASSISTANCE IN THE BATTLE

God is willing and able to help us through our problems. We just have to ask Him and then align our thinking with His in three ways:

Realize that the battle is not ours, but God's.

Jennifer Rundle put her life in God's hands and then waited patiently for Him to heal her. On May 13, 1983, four days after her eighteenth birthday, she had surgery to remove the tumor, which had grown to the size of a grapefruit and was nestled against an artery. Positioned as it was next to some lymph nodes, the cancer had had every opportunity to spread throughout her bloodstream—particularly since it had festered undetected for five years. To the doctors' amazement, though, they could find no traces of the cancer in her blood or anywhere else in her body. The nature of cancer is to grow, but as they put it, "Somehow, this tumor contained itself."[3] The doctors were able to remove all of it.

God had answered her prayers for healing; He had performed a miracle in this battle with cancer. He was a name that had answered her every need.

Recognize human limitations and allow God's strength to work through our fears and weaknesses.

During a time of suffering, both Peter and Paul advise us to commit our pain and suffering to God, realizing He is faithful to work out all things for good and God's glory (Romans 8:28; 1 Peter 4:19).

Jennifer Rundle never gave up. She said that God would heal her, she taped His promises on the walls, and she held on to His strength to overcome her natural fear. When she was asked which miracle in her healing clinched her awareness of God's intervention in her life, she replied without hesitation, "Of course, I am so grateful that God healed me. The real miracle that gave my life new hope lies in how God used cancer for His glory. When I got home from the hospital I wrote down all the ways He was glorified—and I counted more than sixty-five different items."[4]

Ask God for help in our daily battles.

When Jennifer was released from the hospital, she still wore a bag on her stomach to aid in digestion—and the doctors warned that it would be two or three months before her colon was ready to work on its own. Two or three months? Her parents' house was only a mile from the ocean, and summertime was just around the corner. Jennifer hated the thought of missing out on all the fun her friends would have at the beach.

Two and a half weeks after her cancer surgery, she went back to the doctor. He examined her, dumbfounded. "I certainly can't explain it," he admitted, "but your colon is completely ready to go!"[5]

Jennifer Rundle's story is told in her sister's book, *A Celebration of Miracles*, which presents a variety of stories—from a missionary surrounded by murdering bandits to a baby faced with a life-threatening tumor. And even in their diversity the miracles proclaim a common and unmistakable message: God knows our needs, and He is willing and able to meet them.

Reflecting on God's goodness, Jennifer made a startling observation: "Even with the physical pain, this has been one of the best times in my life."[6] Jennifer came to know God as her healer.

FIFTEEN ATTRIBUTES OF THE LORD

Look up the Scriptures below and write them in the space provided. Then read them *aloud,* because "faith comes by hearing, and hearing by the word of God" (Romans 10:17). In the days ahead choose at least one name that is applicable to your needs and frequently thank God that He is that for you. Keep in mind that everything about His personality is stronger than anything negative in yours.

1. He is my Restorer (Psalm 23:3).

2. He is my Helper (John 14:16).

3. He is my Strength (Isaiah 12:2).

4. He is my Hope (Psalm 71:5).

5. He is my Resting Place (Jeremiah 50:6).

6. He is my Fortress (Psalm 18:2).

7. He is my Refuge from the storm (Isaiah 25:4).

8. He is my Everlasting Father (Isaiah 9:6).

9. He is my Deliverer (Psalm 70:5).

10. He is my Counselor (Psalm 16:7).

11. He is my Healer (Malachi 4:2).

12. He is my Shield (Psalm 33:20).

13. He is my Hiding Place (Psalm 32:7).

14. He is my Shade from the heat (Isaiah 25:4).

15. He is my Stronghold in the day of trouble (Nahum 1:7).

PART TWO
The Solid Foundation

CHAPTER EIGHT

Praying to Move on with the Lord

EVERY WEEK I HEARD PASTOR JACK PREACH ABOUT "MOVING ON with the Lord." Each time he mentioned it, he waved his arm slowly across the congregation, like a shepherd trying to move his sheep in a certain direction. One morning as he waved his arm over the congregation, I realized that you don't just stay in one place after you receive the Lord. You have to start growing.

The truth is, I had made it into eternity by securing life after death. However, my life here on earth still needed work. I had to do certain things daily to sustain life and become spiritually and emotionally healthy. What a revelation!

Over the next few months I learned about five key elements—spiritual building blocks—that will strengthen our relationship with God:

- The Word of God
- Prayer
- Praise
- Confession
- Ongoing forgiveness

These building blocks are essential to having a solid foundation in His truth. By neglecting even one of them, we end up with cracks in our foundation. In this part of the book we will look at each of these key elements.

Some people do "get by," never doing any of these things, but I wasn't interested in getting by. I'd been doing that for years. I wanted true spiritual well-being and a sense of purpose and direction. I wanted God's will for my life.

These key elements must be part of our daily lives. Sometimes we think, *I confessed my past errors at the beginning of my walk with the Lord, so I don't need to confess again—unless I rob a bank or kill someone.* Yet confession is really a way of life. If we're not walking God's way, if we're doing anything in disobedience—gossiping, lying, or speaking in a degrading manner to someone—we need to clear the slate, and that only comes with confession: *God, I come before You and I confess my attitude toward my boss. I repent of that attitude. I want to become more like Christ every day.*

Confession is the one of the five keys that I often used to forget. Sometimes when my husband, Michael, would say something that hurt my feelings, I would react—and say something equally as offensive back. This only made the strife worse. I soon learned that before I apologized to Michael, I had to apologize to God. I would go before the Lord and say, "God, I'm sorry for what I said. I know I was moving in the flesh and not the Spirit." I found that confessing to the Lord helped me to stop the behavior and be able to apologize to Michael with a better attitude.

Think about your own life. Has anything like that happened between you and another person? Do you have any attitude that you need to confess? If so, don't hesitate. The sooner you take care of it the better.

Take an inventory of your present life:

Do you read the Bible daily?

Do you pray about all things?

Do you praise God at times during the day?

Do you confess to Him immediately when you know you have violated His laws?

Are you able to forgive those who hurt you?

If you answered no to any of the above questions, do not be discouraged. This part of the book will help you grow in these areas.

In the space below, write a prayer to the Lord, asking Him to help you remember the importance of His Word, prayer, praise, confession, and ongoing forgiveness in your daily walk with Him.

FIVE SPIRITUAL BUILDING BLOCKS

As you begin this study of the five key elements—the spiritual building blocks—that will strengthen your relationship with God, look up a passage of Scripture that speaks of each one and write it in the space below. You will not be able to write all the verses of the longer passages; just note the verses that mean the most to you. Then work through the questions.

1. The Word of God (Read Mark 4:3–20, The Parable of the Soils)

Three of the four types of people represented in this parable are examples of:

What keeps the word from bearing fruit in each example?

- The seed sown by the wayside:

- The seed sown on stony ground:

- The seed sown among thorns:

Why does the word sown on good ground endure?

What is the promise to you if you are one of these people?

2. Prayer (Read Psalm 66:16–20)

When might the Lord refuse to hear the psalmist's prayer?

What has the psalmist's experience been, however?

What is a prerequisite to your prayer being heard?

3. Praise (Read Exodus 15:1–5)

Why are the Israelites praising God?

What attributes are they praising Him for?

Have you recognized these attributes in your life?

4. Confession (Read Romans 14:11–12)

Who shall give an account to God?

5. Ongoing forgiveness (Read 2 Chronicles 7:14)

CHAPTER NINE

Praying for a Solid Foundation in God's Truth

EARLY IN MY SPIRITUAL JOURNEY I LEARNED THAT THERE IS NO way to walk as a Christian if we don't read the instruction manual, the Bible. When I first became a Christian I relied on Pastor Hayford's preaching to tell me how to live each day. He asked us to bring a Bible to church with us, and I thought all I had to do was follow along as he mentioned the Scripture that was important to his teaching for that service.

One day, when Pastor Jack was encouraging us to "move on" in our spiritual walks by reading the Bible, I realized that he was asking us to read the Bible each day by ourselves.

WHAT? ME, READ?

You might feel as I did. Read the Bible, each day, by myself? I'm not so sure about that.

In *Praying God's Will for Your Life,* I listed fifteen reasons to read the Bible daily. Seven of those reasons came from one particular psalm, Psalm 119, the longest psalm and the longest chapter in the Bible (176 verses in all). And the entire theme of this psalm is: God's Word is true and wonderful.

The psalm is an acrostic of twenty-two sections, each one corresponding to a letter of the Hebrew alphabet.[1] If you knew these ABCs, you could easily memorize this psalm, even though it is so long. And the psalm is also repetitive, but for a good reason; the author wants to reinforce over and over again the importance of reading God's Word.

Let's look at parts of this psalm together, concentrating on the sections that answer the question "Why should I read the Bible daily?"

To Shape Yourself and Your Life Correctly

The second stanza, the *beth* of the Hebrew alphabet, begins with a question: "How can a young person stay pure?"[2] And the answer is immediate: "By obeying your word and following its rules" (v. 9 NLT).

The author goes on to say, "I have hidden your word in my heart, that I might not sin against you" (v. 11).

In the third stanza the writer tells why we need God's guidance: "I am but a foreigner here on earth," he says (v. 19). So are we. We are creatures made in heaven, whose destination is heaven, and whose time on this earth is brief in the timeline of eternity. We are more heavenly beings than earthlings. But if we want to stay away from sin, if we want to become all God has created us to be, we need to read God's Word, His instruction book while we're here.

To Have Strength, Comfort, and Hope

The fourth stanza, the *daleth* of the Hebrew alphabet, describes our condition: "I lie in the dust, completely discouraged" (v. 25). The antidote? God's Word. The psalmist pleads with God, "Revive me by your word" (v. 25). Late in this stanza he says, "I weep with grief; encourage me by your word" (v. 28).

And he repeats this thought in stanza 7, the *zain* of the Hebrew alphabet: "Your promise revives me: it comforts me in all my troubles" (v. 50).

God's Word gives us strength, comfort, and hope. And His Word also helps us to distinguish good from evil.

To Distinguish Good from Evil

In the thirteenth stanza, the *mem* of the Hebrew alphabet, the writer claims to have more insight than his teachers because "I have refused to walk on any path of evil, that I may remain obedient to your word" (v. 101). The Bible can help all of us—young and old alike, Bible teacher and student, layman and clergy—to separate good from evil in our daily lives. God does not believe in an elite, country-club Christianity. Instead He reaches out to all His children through His Word.

To Have Direction and to Know God's Will

Stanza fourteen, *nun* in the Hebrew alphabet, begins with a very familiar verse: "Your word is a lamp for my feet and a light for my path" (v. 105). Just as we need a flashlight to see at night when the light is gone, we need God's Word to light our way in a dark world. We can know God's will for our lives if we read the Bible daily. Then we will be able to see clearly.

By the fourteenth stanza the author of Psalm 119 has given us four good reasons to read the Bible: to shape yourself and your life correctly; to have strength, comfort, and hope; to distinguish good from evil; and to have direction and know God's will. In stanza 21 he adds a fifth: to be rid of anxiety and have peace.

To Be Rid of Anxiety and to Have Peace

The psalmist begins stanza 21, the *schin* of the Hebrew alphabet, with the statement "Powerful people harass me without cause" (v. 161), giving one reason he has been deprived of peace. Only four verses later he assures us, "Those who love your law have great peace and do not stumble" (v. 165).

Who does not long for peace in our troubled world, both between nations and within ourselves? Worldwide peace is probably unattainable, but internal peace is promised throughout the Bible for those who follow God's Word.

Those are just five reasons to read the Bible daily. The other ten reasons are listed on pages 89–90. Look up the Scriptures and write them in the spaces below each citation. And be sure to read Psalm 119 in its entirety before you reach a final conclusion.

Perhaps you wonder as I did at one point, *How can I be sure that the Bible is really God's Word?* Let me give you a few reasons.

IS THE BIBLE REALLY GOD'S WORD?

Evidence for a positive answer to the question, Is the Bible really God's Word? is both internal, within the Bible itself, and external.

Internal Evidence

Internal evidence can be found both in the Bible's claims about itself and also in the number of prophecies from the Old Testament that are fulfilled in the New.

The Bible's Claims About Itself. From a cold Roman cell the apostle Paul witnessed to Timothy, his disciple, about the truth of the Bible. Just before his death, he said, "All Scripture is given by inspiration of God, and is profitable for doctrine, for reproof, for correction, for instruction in righteousness, that the man of God may be complete, thoroughly equipped for every good work" (2 Timothy 3:16).

A man who is facing death rarely lies. In this second letter to Timothy, Paul is trying to impart the most important truths of the Christian faith so that his disciple will carry on the work Paul has begun.

Prophecies Fulfilled. In the chart below I will mention six prophecies of the Messiah from the Old Testament that are fulfilled by Jesus Christ in the New Testament. Actually scholars have mentioned forty-four in all, which are described on pages 1549–1554 of *The New Open Bible.*[3] (All of the Scriptures in the chart below are presented in the King James Version.)

I have purposely picked Scriptures that neither the writers of the Old Testament nor Jesus Christ had control over; these occurrences were influenced by outside forces. And all of these prophecies in the Old Testament were fulfilled by Jesus hundreds of years later.

Subject	Prophetic Scripture	Fulfilled
1. Born in Bethlehem	Micah 5:2 But thou, Bethlehem Ephratah, though thou be little among the thousands of Judah, yet out of thee shall he come forth unto me that is to be ruler in Israel: whose goings	Luke 2:4–5, 7 And Joseph also went up from Galilee out of the city of Nazareth, into Judaea, unto the city of David, which is called Bethlehem; (because he was of the house and

Subject	Prophetic Scripture	Fulfilled
	forth have been from of old, from everlasting.	lineage of David,) to be taxed with Mary his espoused wife, being great with child. . . . And she brought forth her firstborn son, and wrapped him in swaddling clothes, and laid him in a manger; because there was no room for them in the inn.
2. Born of a virgin	Isaiah 7:14 Therefore the Lord himself shall give you a sign; behold, a virgin shall conceive, and bear a son, and shall call his name Immanuel.	Luke 1:26–27, 30–31 And in the sixth month the angel Gabriel was sent from God unto a city of Galilee, named Nazareth, to a virgin espoused to a man whose name was Joseph, of the house of David; and the virgin's name was Mary. And the angel said unto her, Fear not, Mary: for thou hast found favour with God. And, behold, thou shalt conceive in thy womb, and bring forth a son, and shalt call his name JESUS.

Subject	Prophetic Scripture	Fulfilled
3. Rejected by His own people, the Jews	Isaiah 53:3 He is despised and rejected of men; a man of sorrows, and acquainted with grief; and we hid as it were our faces from him; he was despised, and we esteemed him not.	John 1:11 He came unto his own, and his own received him not. Luke 23:18 And they cried out all at once, saying, Away with this man, and release unto us Barabbas.
4. Betrayed by a close friend	Psalm 41:9 Yea, mine own familiar friend, in whom I trusted, which did eat of my bread, hath lifted up his heel against me.	Luke 22:47–48 And while he yet spake, behold a multitude, and he that was called Judas, one of the twelve, went before them, and drew near unto Jesus to kiss him. But Jesus, said unto him, Judas, betrayest thou the Son of man with a kiss?
5. Betrayed for thirty pieces of silver	Zechariah 11:12 And I said unto them, If ye think good, give me my price; and if not, forbear. So they weighed for my price thirty pieces of silver.	Matthew 26:14–15 Then one of the twelve, called Judas Iscariot, went unto the chief-priests. And said unto them, What will ye give me, and I will deliver him unto you? And they covenanted with him for thirty pieces of silver.

Subject	Prophetic Scripture	Fulfilled
6. Soldiers gambled for His garment	Psalm 22:17–18 I may tell all my bones: they look and stare upon me. They part my garments among them, and cast lots upon my vesture.	Matthew 27:35 And they crucified him, and parted his garments, casting lots:

External Evidence

A court case can also be made for the truth of the Bible from external evidence. First from archaeological digs.

Archaeological Digs. In his book *The New Evidence That Demands a Verdict,* Josh McDowell quotes Nelson Glueck, the renowned Jewish archaeologist, who wrote: "It may be stated categorically that no archaeological discovery has ever controverted a biblical reference."[4]

McDowell also talks about the incredible accuracy of the gospel of Luke. At one time people doubted the events surrounding Jesus' birth in this gospel. "Critics argued that there was no census, that Quirinius was not governor of Syria at that time, and that everyone did not have to return to his ancestral home."[5]

But archaeological discoveries have instead proven the accuracy of this Gospel's account of Christ's birth.

First of all, archaeological discoveries show that the Romans had a regular enrollment of taxpayers and also held censuses every fourteen years. This procedure was indeed begun under Augustus and the first took place in either 23–22 B.C. or in 9–8 B.C. The latter would be the one to which Luke refers.

Second, we find evidence that Quirinius was governor of Syria around 7 B.C. This assumption is based on an inscription found in Antioch ascribing to Quirinius this post. As a result of this finding, it is now supposed that he was governor twice—once in 7 B.C. and the other time in 6 A.D. (the date ascribed by Josephus).

Last, in regard to the practices of enrollment, a papyrus found in Egypt gives directions for the conduct of a census. It reads: "Because of the approaching census it is necessary that all those residing for any cause away from their homes should at once prepare to return to their own governments in order that they may complete the family registration of the enrollment and that the tilled lands may retain those belonging to them."[6]

Without doubt archaeology substantiated the Bible's account of Christ's birth.

Another archaeological find, the Dead Sea Scrolls, further substantiates the Bible. McDowell says, "If you had asked any biblical scholar, before the discovery of the Dead Sea Scrolls, what would constitute his dream for a discovery that would greatly verify the reliability of the Old Testament, he or she would have said, 'Older witnesses to the original Old Testament manuscripts.'"[7]

That's just what happened when the Dead Sea Scrolls were discovered in 1947. The scrolls, made up of some 40,000 inscribed fragments, were recorded by the religious community of Qumran on the shores of the Dead Sea. These scrolls not only shed light on this second-century B.C. to first-century A.D. religious community (writings include their "Rule of the Community" and their "Manual of Discipline"), but some of the scrolls are also copies of the Old Testament text dating from more than a century *before* the birth of Christ.[8]

All of these facts—both internal and external—add credence to the Bible. And the contemporary evidence of the Bible's power to change people's lives adds further credibility.

Changes in People's Lives. In the book *Praise Him!*, Les Sussman asked music stars to share their favorite verses from the Bible. Rich Mullins cited Ecclesiastes 7:16–18:

> Be not righteous over much; neither make thyself over wise: why shouldest thou destroy thyself?
>
> Be not over much wicked, neither be thou foolish: why shouldest thou die before thy time?
>
> It is good that thou shouldest take hold of this; yea, also from this withdraw not thine hand; for he that feareth God shall come forth of them all. (KJV)[9]

As I mentioned in Chapter 3, Rich Mullins struggled with addictions and "feeling tormented all the time." Rich found Scripture an antidote to the depression that plagued him. He told the reporter, "This scripture has come into play so many times in my life when I've fallen into those moods and the temptation of evaluating myself and saying 'How am I doing?' It seems that God is always saying 'I'm not worried so much about how you're doing as much as I'm glad about who you are.' . . . I read the Bible because I'll find God there. It's about a daily walk with this person Jesus."[10]

If you wish to have this kind of a daily walk with Jesus, begin tomorrow to read the Bible daily. If the version of the Bible you're reading is difficult to understand, get another translation. In addition to the King James Version, I have used the New King James, the New International Version, and the New Living Translation in this book; other versions, such as the New American Standard or the Amplified Bible, are also easy to read.

Some of the insights I have shared with you in this workbook have come from the notes in *The New Open Bible*. If you are purchasing a Bible, glance through some pages to see if there are notes throughout the Bible to clarify Scripture for you. Study editions and life application editions usually have this added benefit.

God promises to bless you if you "abide" in His Word. Write your name in the Scripture promise below and know that this is truly His will for you.

If you, _____, abide in Me, and My words abide in you, you will ask what you desire, and it shall be done for you. (John 15:7)

Then give the Lord a promise in return. Vow to sit at the knee of your Maker daily as you read His Word.

TEN REASONS TO READ THE BIBLE DAILY

Begin this exercise by reading Psalm 119 in its entirety. Then look up the Scriptures that testify to the power of prayer and write them in the spaces below. As you do so, watch the Lord confirm the importance of daily Bible reading in your heart. Finally write the Scriptures that are most significant to you on an index card that you carry in your purse or place on your vanity mirror.

1. To have more in this life (Psalm 119:50)

2. To be able to see clearly (Psalm 119:130)

3. To set things right when life is out of control (Psalm 19:7–8)

4. To experience healing and deliverance (Psalm 107:20)

5. To grow in the Lord (1 Peter 2:2)

6. To know what's really in your heart (Hebrews 4:12)

7. To build faith (Romans 10:17)

8. To have joy (Psalm 16:11)

9. To understand God's power (John 1:3)

10. To understand God's love for you (John 1:14)

CHAPTER TEN

Praying to Know the Power of Prayer

PAT AND SHIRLEY BOONE HAVE BEEN MICHAEL'S AND MY FRIENDS since the seventies when we attended Bible studies at their home. We also knew their four daughters and their families. One night in 2001 we received a call from friends of the Boone family, asking us to pray for the Boones' grandson, Ryan, who had fallen through a roof skylight to a concrete basement four floors below. At first the paramedics had thought this 210-pound college student was dead, but Ryan survived the accident because he hit stair rails on the way down. He suffered massive injuries to his body—but his life was spared. Still many people felt Ryan's condition was hopeless.

My heart was broken for the family. I knew how devastated I would be if this had happened to our son, Chris, who is exactly the same age as Ryan. I fell to my knees in prayer, and then called my prayer group and other friends to pray as well. Many other people who knew the Boones were also notified, and soon thousands of people around the world were praying for Ryan.

Not long after the accident I ended up sitting beside Pat on a flight to Los Angeles. As we talked about the accident, Pat's faith was obvious—as was his tremendous love for his grandson. He told me how the prayers of so many people were giving the Boone family great hope.

For five weeks Ryan lay unconscious, attached to a respirator and other life support systems, with little hope for recovery. How difficult it must have been for Ryan's mom and dad, Lyndie and Doug, and his grandparents, aunts, uncles, cousins, and fiancée to see him this way. He had been a vibrant, athletic, godly young man who was not living a wild life and did not deserve what had happened.

Finally the doctors suggested that the time might come when his parents would want to take him off of the life support system. Their prognosis: Ryan would probably remain in a vegetative state.

The Boone family understood the doctor's prognosis, but they also knew the power of prayer. Pat suggested, "You're the medical team; we're the faith team. Let's work together."

On July 26, 2001, Pat Boone appeared on Larry King's television show and asked listeners to pray for Ryan. Millions around the world responded to Pat's plea, including President George and Laura Bush.

On January 24, 2002, Pat Boone returned to Larry's show with his daughter, Lyndie, and films of Ryan in the rehabilitation center. Viewers saw a handsome dark-haired young man who was now able to eat, to squeeze his grandfather's hand, and to kiss his mom and grandfather. This is a testimony to the power of prayer.

"He's gone way beyond what the doctors expected," Pat Boone said. "He's recovered from his coma because he does things now that people in comas don't do . . . He's so close to talking to us.

". . . He's not all the way back yet," Pat said on the program. "It is a process. We can tell he's trying from within. He's cognitive enough now that he understands certain words. And when Lyndie or others give him a command or offer him something to eat, he opens his mouth."

Pat Boone and his family believe in the power of prayer. And so do I. I've seen God's response to my prayers in so many ways, a number of which I've described in my books *The Power of a Praying Wife* and *The Power of a Praying Parent*. But I, like some of you, began my walk with prayer as an adult.

In those early years I came across the Scripture that says, "For your Father knows the things you have need of before you ask Him" (Matthew 6:8). This puzzled me, so I questioned Pastor Jack about it. "If God already knows what I need, why do I even need to ask for anything?"

I told of this conversation in *Praying God's Will for Your Life*. I repeat it here because I believe it is so important to a true understanding of prayer. Pastor Jack responded to my question by saying, "Because God has given us a free will. He has set it up so that we always have a choice about everything we do, including whether or not we choose to communicate with Him. He will never intervene where a man does not want Him.

"God *knows* our thoughts," Pastor Jack continued, "but He *responds* to our prayers. We have to come to a place of realizing that prayer is a *privilege* that is always *ours*, but the *power* in prayer is always His. *Without God, we can't do it. Without us, God won't do it.*"

That put a whole new perspective on prayer for me, and I hope it also helps you to better understand the importance of this conversation between us and our Father.

HOW TO PRAY EFFECTIVELY

We can't receive God's best for our lives, and we can't push back the things that were never God's will for us, except through prayer. Pastor Jack says, "Prayer is not the mystical experience of a few special people, but an aggressive act . . . an act that may be performed by anyone who will accept the challenge to learn to pray."

In Psalm 27 King David says, "My heart has heard you say, 'Come and talk with me.' And my heart responds, 'LORD, I am coming'" (Psalm 27:8 NLT). Can you respond as David did? Can you say, "Lord, I am coming"?

If you have any doubts about the importance of prayer or if you are still praying on an on-again/off-again basis, go through the fifteen reasons to pray on pages 98–99. Select two or three that are most meaningful to you and copy them on index cards to carry in your purse or tape to a mirror to remind you how important it is to pray.

Our friend Screwtape knew how important prayer was. He advised Wormwood about how to obstruct this process: "The best thing, where it is possible, is to keep the patient from the serious intention of praying altogether. When the patient is an adult recently reconverted to the Enemy's party, like your man, this is best done by encouraging him to remember, or to think he remembers, the parrotlike nature of prayers in childhood."[1]

93

As I began my own prayer walk, Pastor Jack encouraged me to pray, just as if God were sitting there with me—and we were having a conversation together. I always try to secure a specific place and a specific time to pray. If you are a morning person, mornings can be best. If you stay up late at night, you may decide on evenings. Either early in the morning or late at night can be moments when other people are not close by so you may have uninterrupted time. Write down what time you believe would work best for you: _____.

A special place is also important. Jesus told His disciples:

> But you, when you pray, you shall not be like the hypocrites. For they love to pray standing in the synagogues and on the corners of the streets, that they may be seen by men. Assuredly, I say to you, they have their reward. But you, when you pray, go into your room, and when you have shut your door, pray to your Father who is in the secret place: and your Father who sees in secret will reward you openly. (Matthew 6:5–6)

Again the objective should be to avoid distractions. Think about your home and note your special prayer place:_____.

Try this for a while, and if it doesn't work, try something else.

It helps to include certain key points in my prayer times. As you begin to pray daily, use these eight areas as an outline. Begin right now by writing your prayers in each area for today:

1. Tell the Lord how much you love Him.

2. Thank Him for all He has done for you.

3. State how dependent you are upon Him.

4. Tell Him everything that's in your heart.

5. Confess anything that needs to be confessed.

6. Give Him all your requests.

7. Wait for Him to speak to your heart. Then record what you hear Him saying:

8. Praise Him for working powerfully in your life.

As you pray be careful not to judge the power of your prayers by your own feelings. This can also be a tool the enemy uses against us. Screwtape advised Wormwood:

> Whenever they are attending to the Enemy Himself we are defeated, but there are ways of preventing them from doing so. The simplest is to turn their gaze away from Him towards themselves. Keep them watching their own minds and trying to produce *feelings* there by the action of their own wills . . . When they say they are praying for forgiveness, let them be trying to feel forgiven. Teach them to estimate the value of each prayer by their success in producing the desired feeling; and never let them suspect how much success or failure of that kind depends on whether they are well or ill, fresh or tired, at the moment.[2]

Let Screwtape's advice to Wormwood be a warning to you. When you pray, concentrate on the Lord Jesus Christ and not on your emotions. Eliphaz, one of the three friends who tries to help Job understand what had happened to him, told Job what would happen if he delighted himself in the Almighty and looked up to God: "You will pray to him, and he will hear you, and you will fulfill your vows to him. Whatever you decide to do will be accomplished, and light will shine on the road ahead of you" (Job 22:27–30 NLT).

And in the future, look for some other strong believers to join you in prayer. Your spiritual well-being depends upon two kinds of regular prayer. One is deep, intimate prayer alone—just you and God. The other is prayer with other believers—praying for one another. The Bible says, "Where two or three are gathered together in My name, I am there in the midst of them" (Matthew 18:20).

See if your church has Bible-study groups, prayer groups, or home groups and join one. Or ask God to lead you to at least one other believer, and be bold enough to ask that person if he or she wants to pray with you regularly. Fill that person's name in here: _____.

Now be specific about when you will approach that person: _____.

DOES GOD ALWAYS HEAR MY PRAYERS?

The answer to the question "Does God always hear my prayers?" is a resounding yes! He certainly has heard mine over the years. As Pastor Jack Hayford so succinctly puts it, "Your heavenly Father is waiting to hear from you. Call home!"

Don't allow discouragement over unanswered prayer to cause you to doubt that God has heard you. If you have received Jesus and are praying in His name, then God hears you, and something is happening whether you see it right away or not.

When Pat Boone appeared on *Larry King Live*, he said that people might wonder "If God is so powerful, why didn't He heal Ryan right away?" instead of such a gradual process. "God's not a short-order cook," Pat said. "God's a Father. We're created in His image. And when something like this happens He puts His arm around us and says, "Okay, we've got a problem, don't we. What can you do about it? Let's see what you can do, son or daughter. And then I'll show you what to do, and then when you've run out of your abilities, I'll kick in. But let's do this together. And not just you, but friends, family, people across this television network."

None of us will stop praying for Ryan until we see him completely restored. If you feel so inclined, please pray with us for Ryan too. There is power in numbers of people praying.

Journaling your prayers is powerful too. I've included a prayer journal at the back of this book for that purpose. List your prayer requests in this journal and date them. Then when one is answered, record the date and how God answered this prayer. As you see your prayers being answered, your faith in the power of prayer will grow, just as mine did. I hope that many of us will be able to enter the date when our prayers have been answered for Ryan's complete healing.

You should also consider praying for our president and our nation's leaders.

THE PRESIDENTIAL PRAYER TEAM

After the terrible tragedy on September 11, 2001, I was asked to become an Honorary Committee Member of the Presidential Prayer Team. "Yes," I immediately replied. "I want to be a part of this." I was already praying for the president and his staff anyway, and I was glad to join with other Christians to pray in an organized way so we might intercede with great power.

Periodically President Bush talks with the leaders of this prayer team and gives them his requests, which are then e-mailed to all of us on the prayer team each week. It's a great spiritual connection to know the heart of the president and to be able to pray for his greatest needs.

When the prayer team first started there were only a few of us; now over a million Americans have committed to pray for the president each week. If you would like to add your name to this list, just go to this Web site:

http://www.presidentialprayerteam.org/register.asp

If we all pray together I believe we will see the hand of God affect our nation as never before. And not only that, we can positively affect the nations of the world. Join me in watching for answers in the days and months and years ahead.

FIFTEEN REASONS TO PRAY

Look up the Scriptures that testify to the power of prayer and write them in the spaces below. As you do so, watch the Lord confirm the importance of prayer in your heart. Then write the Scriptures that are most significant to you on an index card that you carry in your purse or place on your mirror.

1. To seek the face of the Lord and know Him better (Psalm 27:8)

2. To get your eyes off your problems and onto the Lord (Psalm 121:1)

3. To speak to God (1 Peter 3:12)

4. To unburden your heart (Psalm 142:1–2)

5. To make your requests known to God (Matthew 21:22)

6. To hear God (Proverbs 8:32–34)

7. To be free of suffering (James 5:13)

8. To resist temptation (Matthew 26:41)

9. To be rescued from distress (Psalm 107:19)

10. To receive God's reward (Matthew 6:6)

11. To withstand evil (Ephesians 6:13)

12. To have joy (John 16:24)

13. To get close to God (Isaiah 64:7)

14. To be healed emotionally (James 5:13)

15. To have peace (Philippians 4:6–7)

CHAPTER ELEVEN

Praying to Understand the Freedom in Praise

MERLIN CAROTHERS'S BOOK *PRISON TO PRAISE* WAS ONE OF THE first books I read after I became a Christian. This book changed my life because it had never occurred to me to praise God in the middle of difficult situations.

Carothers was a chaplain in the U.S. Army who had an unusual career. He began as an enlisted man, a private who hungered to join our forces in Europe during the Second World War. Carothers trained at Fort Benning, Georgia, and when he seemed to be stalled there, he and a friend "jumped fence," stole a car, and began a journey to freedom, they thought. In a short period of time they were caught as they attempted to rob a store to obtain money.

Carothers's story began in prison, but it ended in praise as a servant of God, a chaplain. After his circuitous route during the Second World War, he attended a church service with his grandparents and heard God speaking to him. At the end of the service he went forward for the altar call, a mixed blessing for his grandfather, who had been sitting beside Carothers, praying, "God, if You'll change Merlin, I'll give up my chewing and smoking even if it kills me." God answered this grandfather's prayer, and he responded by giving up his use of tobacco.

After this call on Merlin's life, he went to seminary, returned to the army as a chaplain, and served God there for many years, part of the time in Vietnam. When he returned to Fort Benning, he experienced days of discouragement. Twenty-three years earlier he had been in the stockade there as a prisoner. He returned as a chaplain, which was an exciting challenge, but he was all too aware of his own shortcomings. Knowing this was not God's will for him, he began a study of the Scriptures. In John 17 he read that Jesus prayed for His followers, " . . . that they may have My joy fulfilled in themselves" (v. 13). In the parable of the talents in Matthew 25:21, he read, "You were faithful over a few things, I will make you ruler over many things. Enter into the joy of your Lord."[1]

Many other Scriptures spoke of the "joy of the Lord" but Carothers was locked in depression. Was there a scriptural reason?

Then Merlin read Paul's second letter to the Corinthians. In chapter 12 Paul says, "Therefore most gladly I will rather boast in my infirmities, that the power of Christ may rest upon me. Therefore I take pleasure in infirmities, in reproaches, in needs, in persecutions, in distresses, for Christ's sake. For when I am weak, then I am strong" (vv. 9–10).

Carothers, like many of us, knew he didn't rejoice in infirmities. Yet over and over again in the Bible he read words that suggested he should thank God—praise Him—for everything.

In the next weeks Carothers practiced this principle. He thanked God for the opportunity to get up in the morning, even though he always wished to stay in bed just five more minutes. He thanked God for his allergies, for his painful headaches. He thanked the Lord when his car wouldn't start morning after morning, threatening to make him late for work.

And he said these verses from 1 Thessalonians 5 over and over to himself: "Rejoice always, pray without ceasing, in everything give thanks; for this is the will of God in Christ Jesus for you" (vv. 16–18). And in each of the above instances, which were difficulties for him, God turned the problems around.

Carothers shared these experiences, and those of other people he later helped by applying this principle, in his book *Prison to Praise*, which was published in 1970. As far as I know he was a pioneer in understanding the power of praise, which opens the door for God to work in our lives.[2]

Praise is not always my first reaction to things, however, so I often have to remind myself of Pastor Jack Hayford's teaching on praise. He said, "It's not your saying, 'I'll give it everything I've got and the Lord will bless it,' but rather it's the Lord saying to you, 'You just bless My name and I'll give it everything I have.'"

Without praise we experience an eroding in our spirit that leads to bondage and death. The Bible says, "Although they knew God, they did not glorify Him as God, nor were thankful, but became *futile* in their *thoughts*, and their foolish *hearts* were *darkened*" (Romans 1:21, emphasis added).

Merlin Carothers says, "Very often it is our attitudes that hinder the solution of a problem. God is sovereign and could certainly cut across our wrong thought patterns and attitudes. But His perfect plan is to bring each of us into fellowship and communion with Him, and so He allows circumstances and incidents which will bring our wrong attitudes to our attention."[3]

Now when I come to the place where my flesh can't go any further, I stop where I am and worship God.

A KEY TO TRANSFORMATION

Worship is powerful because God's presence comes to dwell in our midst when we praise Him, and in His presence we find healing, transformation, and direction for our lives. In fact, the more time we spend praising the Lord, the more we will see ourselves and our circumstances grow in wholeness and completeness. That's because praise softens our hearts and makes them pliable.

Merlin Carothers says, "I have come to believe that the prayer of praise is the highest form of communion with God, and one that always releases a great deal of power into our lives. Praising Him is not something we do because we feel good; rather it is an act of obedience. Often the prayer of praise is done in sheer teeth-gritting willpower; yet when we persist in it, somehow the power of God is released into us and into the situation. At first in a trickle perhaps, but later in a growing stream that finally floods us and washes away old hurts and scars."[4]

In the Old Testament the people who carried the ark of the covenant stopped every six steps to worship God. We, too, need to remind ourselves not to go very far without stopping to worship. For spiritual well-being, we have to frequently stop to praise God for who He is and what He has done in our lives.

Now is the time to start being thankful to God for everything in your life. Jennifer Rundle, the high school senior who was diagnosed with colon cancer, says, "I believe the key to my healing was being thankful. Before my parents and I began to see God work miracles, I had to exchange my plans for His. I dropped my plans to go to the prom, to get out of the hospital. And then we asked God, 'What do *You* want to do?' That day I not only became willing to be in the hospital for His glory, but I was also thankful. It was an honor to be part of God's will."

I have listed fifteen reasons to praise the Lord at the end of this chapter. You will notice that all of these reasons are found in the psalms, most of which were written by King David. And unlike the other biblical passages I have listed, these are often entire chapters, rather than selected verses. You obviously cannot copy the entire psalm. But do read the entire psalm and note the verses or thoughts that bless you the most. As you write these Scripture verses, watch the Lord confirm the importance of praising Him in your heart.

Merlin Carothers saw many people's lives change as they practiced praising God. One army wife came to see him with a problem that seemed to only be solvable by divorce. Her husband had developed an excessive drinking problem and would often pass out drunk on the living room floor or in the hallway of their apartment. The woman was worried about the effect his drunkenness was having on their teenage children and herself.

She began by telling Carothers, "Whatever you say, Chaplain, don't tell me to stay with him. I just can't do it."

Instead Carothers asked that she thank God that her husband was an alcoholic. As many other people Carothers had advised to thank God in difficult and extreme situations, she thought this sounded ridiculous. Yet she knelt as the chaplain prayed that God would release in her enough faith to believe that He is a God of love and power who holds the universe in His hand.

When Carothers called her two weeks later, the woman told him about the miracle that had occurred. "The day I was in your office he came home from work and for the first time in seven years he didn't go to the refrigerator for a beer. Instead he went into the living room and talked to the children."[5]

And her husband didn't have a drink in the two weeks that followed. The power of praising—and worshiping—God in all circumstances had healed his addiction.

Worship, God's Way

To have spiritual well-being and to know God's will, we must worship God *His* way, which doesn't always fit our schedule or style.

1. *Praise is meant to be sung.* King David says in Psalm 147:1: "It is good to sing praises to our God; for it is pleasant, and praise is beautiful." Some of us may be shy about our musical ability, or we may just not feel like singing. Yet in the Bible the singers went before the troops into battle because their singing of praises to God bolstered the troops and confused the enemy (2 Chronicles 20:20–23). This works exactly the same way for us today.

You may need a good voice—and the ability to read musical notes—to sing in the church choir, but all of us can sing or hum along to hymns or praise songs. And the praise songs are often repetitive and easy to learn. The more you sing them, the more they will stay in your mind.

In my book *Praying God's Will for Your Life,* I suggest that if you are so depressed or hurting that you can't even unclench your jaw (and some of us feel this way at times), begin to hum to the Lord any melody that comes to mind. Then put words to it from your heart. Or open your Bible to one of the psalms in the list of fifteen reasons to praise the Lord at the end of this chapter and sing these words to the melody that you are humming. Or you might put a worship tape into your stereo and simply sing along. I often play a worship CD in my car as I do errands; we can worship God anywhere and at any time.

2. *Praise is meant to be expressed with the lifting of your hands.* "Lift up your hands in the sanctuary, and bless the LORD" (Psalm 134:2). Lifting our hands to the Lord as we praise God is also an act that is not second nature to us. The most important reason for us to do this is to let go of everything we're holding on to and surrender to God: "I give You everything of myself, Lord."

Unfortunately some people feel uncomfortable when other people raise their hands in church. If that's the condition in your church, you may restrict this expression of your love of the Lord to your personal prayer time. But I wonder: Why is it okay to raise our hands at football games and music concerts, but odd to do so in reverence to God? If it feels strange to you, just remember that the more you do it, the more comfortable you will feel.

Some people say this is an emotional expression, rather than an expression of true commitment to Jesus. Yet King David, one of the greatest patriarchs in the Bible, was joyful in his praise to the Lord. And even back then his enthusiasm was questioned—by his wife, Michal (2 Samuel 6:16). That didn't stop David, however, from singing and dancing when the ark of the covenant was returned to Jerusalem. And God did not bless Michal.

3. *Worship is meant to be done with other believers.* Millions of people say the word *hallelujah* when they praise God. This word is an imperative form of the Hebrew verb *halal*, which means "praise." The *hallelu* part of the word is not only a command, but the form is plural in Hebrew, which suggests congregational praise. The book of Psalms contains about a third of these uses, because the psalms are the praises of Israel—and also of the modern church.[6] The Jewish people praised the Lord with music, choirs, congregational singing, dance, and even speaking (Jeremiah 31:7). The earliest recorded song in the Bible is the Song of Moses (Exodus 15), which was sung as the Hebrew people celebrated God's miraculous deliverance from the Egyptian army at the Red Sea.

The Bible tells us that God is blessed by our worship. Imagine that. The almighty, omniscient, omnipotent God is blessed by *us*. Jesus told the Samaritan woman at the well, "But the time is coming and is already here when true worshipers will worship the Father in spirit and in truth. The Father is looking for anyone who will worship him that way" (John 4:23 NLT).

Some people think of God as a distant King, sitting on a throne in heaven, who is so busy taking care of this world, He has little time for individual Christians. Yet our Father is looking for those who will worship Him.

Write a prayer of praise in the space below. Thank God for His mighty power and love. Thank Him that His plans and purposes for you are good. Thank Him that in any weak area of your life, He will be strong. You might even look at the names of the Lord on pages 40–43 and use them in your prayer. For instance, "I praise You, Lord, because You are my Refuge from the storm and my Everlasting Father, my Abba."

Now write a prayer of praise for a difficult situation or person in your life. Thank God for this person or situation. Thank Him that He is a God of love and is all-powerful. Ask Him to help you truly praise Him for this person or situation.

And remember to truly turn this situation over to God. Merlin Carothers says, "Praise is not another way of bargaining with the Lord. We don't say, 'Now we've praised You in the middle of this mess, so get us out of it.'

"Praising God with a pure heart means we must let God cleanse our hearts from impure motives and hidden designs. We have to experience the dying to self so that we can live again in Christ in newness of mind and spirit."[7]

Praise is our greatest weapon against the feelings of anger or inadequacy that undermine all God has made us to be.

FIFTEEN REASONS TO PRAISE THE LORD

Look up the Scriptures that testify to the importance of praising the Lord. Many of the passages below are entire chapters of Scripture, rather than specific verses. Obviously you cannot copy the entire psalm here. Instead note the verses or thoughts that bless you the most. As you write these Scripture verses, watch the Lord confirm the importance of praising Him in your heart.

1. To enthrone God and acknowledge His greatness (Psalm 95:1–5)

2. To increase our awareness of God's presence (Psalm 103)

3. To have the joy of the Lord (Psalm 30)

4. To acknowledge God's hand in every area of our lives (Psalm 91)

5. To release God's power into our situations (Psalm 144)

6. To know God better (Psalm 50:23)

7. To break our chains of bondage and bring deliverance (Psalm 50:14–15)

8. To be under God's covering of safety and protection (Psalm 95:6–7)

9. To strengthen the soul and be transformed (Psalm 138:1–3)

10. To receive guidance and establish God's purposes in our lives (Psalm 16:7–11)

11. To thwart the devil's plans for our destruction (Psalm 92)

12. To dissipate doubt and increase faith (Psalm 27)

13. To be delivered from fear (Psalm 34)

14. To bring a fresh flow of His Holy Spirit in us (Psalm 40)

15. To possess all that God has promised for us (Psalm 147)

CHAPTER TWELVE

Praying for Release from Unconfessed Sin

SOME CHRISTIANS DON'T APPROVE OF THE "OPEN AND POINT method" of reading the Bible as a way to hear from God. I don't believe this is a good way to consistently study the Bible either, but God can sometimes speak to us in this way.

I know of a woman I will call Suzanne who was having difficulty in her relationship with her husband. One night she was awakened, and since she was unable to go back to sleep she went down to the living room and picked up her Bible. At that moment, she used the "open-and-point" method.

Was it a mere coincidence that the Bible opened to Psalm 32? I don't think so. This is what she read.

> When I kept silent, my bones grew old
> Through my groaning all the day long.
> For day and night Your hand was heavy upon me;
> My vitality was turned into the drought
>   of summer. Selah
> I acknowledged my sin to You,
> And my iniquity I have not hidden.

> I said, "I will confess my transgressions to the LORD,"
> And You forgave the iniquity of my sin. (Psalm 32:3–5)

Suzanne felt that God was speaking directly to her through this psalm, which was so appropriate for that night, so she took a long inventory of her relationship with her husband, and she confessed the ways she was at fault to God.

Unconfessed sin affects our whole life. And often we don't recognize it. Yet it becomes a subtle growth, wrapping its tentacles around every part of our being until we are paralyzed. Often we fail to see ourselves as responsible for certain actions. For example, Suzanne realized that she put her husband down by not trusting him to complete something she had asked him to do. And when he made a mistake, she didn't gloss over it, but rolled her eyes in a way that said, "I can't believe you did that!" She knew she was not a supportive wife, and she had read in Christian books that husbands need a lot of affirmation.

Suzanne knew she needed God's help to overcome these hidden faults and she also knew she really hadn't been open to His instruction in the past. She was convicted by the next words of this psalm:

> Do not be like the horse or like the mule,
> Which have no understanding,
> Which must be harnessed with bit and bridle,
> Else they will not come near you. (Psalm 32:9)

Seeing herself as a horse—or worse, a stubborn mule—was not pleasant, but she felt that the description might be accurate.

Take a moment now to make your own private inventory of yourself. Ask God to bring to light sins you are not aware of so that they can be confessed, repented of, and forgiven. Recognize that there is something to confess every day, and pray frequently as King David did: "Cleanse me from secret faults" (Psalm 19:12). Note the faults that come to your mind in the space below:

1. _____

2. _____

3. _____

4. _____

5. _____

THE KEY IS REPENTANCE

For confession to work, repentance must go along with it. Repentance literally means a change of mind. It means to turn your back, walk away, and decide not to do it again.

Take one or more of the faults in the list above and write a prayer of repentance in the space below. Remember to include your desire to turn your back on this sin. Make sure God knows you are truly repentant and ask Him to help you to avoid this tendency in the future.

Sin leads to death; repentance leads to life. The amount of time that passes between the sin and the repentance will account for how much death is reaped in our lives. If this time has been extensive, the problems won't go away immediately when we confess. But our confession starts the process.

There is also much healing when we confess our faults to another person for the purpose of prayer. The Bible says, "Confess your trespasses to one another, and pray for one another, that you may be healed" (James 5:16).

Think about the people you know. Is there someone you can trust with your confession? This must be a person who has the spiritual maturity to not repeat whatever you tell her. Write that person's name here: _____ . What would you like to tell her? _____ .
If you can't think of anyone, ask God to show you who you can trust.

Always keep in mind that God already knows what you have done. Confession is not for Him to find out something. Confession is for *you* to be made whole. As Suzanne read through Psalm 32 that night, she was particularly caught by God's promise in verse 8: "I will instruct you and teach you in the way you should go; I will guide you with My eye."

That night she resolved to be more attuned to God's will for her. She vowed to recognize His presence in every situation. How it must have grieved the Spirit of God to see her treating her husband with disrespect. The Bible says: "Wives, submit to your husbands, as to the Lord. For the husband is head of the wife, as also Christ is head of the church; and He is the Savior of the body. Therefore, just as the church is subject to Christ, so let the wives be to their own husbands in everything" (Ephesians 5:22–24).

Hard words to follow, but ones she felt God was calling her to adopt. Suzanne vowed to soften the parts of her personality that resembled that stubborn mule. And in the next weeks and months she began praying David's prayer at the end of Psalm 19, in which he asked God to cleanse him from his secret faults:

> Let the words of my mouth and the
>   meditation of my heart
> Be acceptable in Your sight,
> O LORD, my strength and my redeemer. (Psalm 19:14)

I suggest that you read this verse again, only this time out loud as a prayer for your life. This would be a good verse to add to your daily prayer time.

Once you have completed this process you should feel more at peace. Suzanne certainly did that night. When she finally went back to bed, she knew that God had dealt with her, just as He wrestled with Jacob in the Bible.

A NEW NAME

God gave many people in the Bible new names. The disciple Peter was named Simon at birth, and Jesus changed his name to Cephas or Peter, which means "rock."[1] When God renamed a person, his or her new name was a symbol of how God changed that individual's life. In the passage below, Jacob, the deceiver, became Israel, the father of the tribes of Israel.

> Then Jacob was left alone; and a Man wrestled with him until the breaking of day.
>   Now when He saw that He did not prevail against him, He touched the

socket of his hip; and the socket of Jacob's hip was out of joint as He wrestled with him.

And He said, "Let Me go, for the day breaks." But he said, "I will not let You go unless You bless me!"

So He said to him, "What is your name?" And he said, "Jacob."

And he said, "Your name shall no longer be called Jacob, but Israel; for you have struggled with God and with men, and have prevailed."

Then Jacob asked Him, saying, "Tell me Your name, I pray." And He said, "Why is it that you ask about My name?" And He blessed him there.

And Jacob called the name of the place Peniel: "For I have seen God face to face, and my life is preserved." (Genesis 21:24–32)

Suzanne knew that during that night with the Lord, her life had also been changed. She wrote the date next to Psalm 32 so that she would not forget that night. And she vowed to pattern her actions closer to God's image than that of a stubborn mule.

THE REMEDY FOR SIN

Look up the Scriptures that show God's plan to remedy our sins and write them in the spaces below. Where an entire chapter of Scripture is indicated, merely note the parts that particularly speak to you.

Romans 5:12–21

Romans 6

1 John 1:9

1 John 2:1–6

GOD'S VIEW OF REPENTANCE

Look up the Scriptures that tell of God's view of repentance and write them in the spaces below.

1. As a necessary part of life
   Romans 2:4

2 Peter 3:9

2. Those who won't repent
   Revelation 9:20–21

   Revelation 16:9–11

We don't have to be one of these sufferers in Revelation. We can repent and be saved.

CHAPTER THIRTEEN

Praying to Forgive Yourself, God, and Others

WHEN SARAH WAS A TEENAGER, HER MOTHER, PEGGY, LEFT HER FATHER after he had experienced several job losses, putting the family in extreme financial straits. Her mom returned home to her own mother's house, where she pursued a degree that would give her the opportunity to earn an income herself. Peggy never filed for separation or divorce.

After Sarah's mom completed her degree, she eventually reunited with her husband, and together they began to rebuild the family's life. But Sarah never forgave her mom for leaving her dad and upsetting the family. The anger grew as Sarah went through her teenage years and exploded into bitter fights and some drinking and rebellion. Worried about her daughter, Peggy went into counseling with Sarah, but Sarah held on to her bitterness toward her mother, which continued to hamper their relationship. Over the years they saw two other counselors, and each time Peggy admitted her own faults and said she was sorry. Yet Sarah never seemed to accept her apology. Today Sarah continues to blame her mother for problems in her own life. She will never be free to move into all God has for her until she completely forgives her mother.

The Stairway to Wholeness

The first step to forgiving is to remember God's forgiveness for the unconfessed sins you brought to Him in the last chapter and sins you mentioned way back in Chapter 3. Let the reality of His forgiveness (Remember He says that your sins have become as white as snow) penetrate the deepest part of your being. Forgiveness is a two-way street. God forgives you, and you forgive others.

Forgiving Others

Forgiveness is a choice we make, not an emotional response. When I say the word *forgiveness*, what is your response? Read the statements below and see if they reflect the way you have felt or feel today. Fill in the blank space if there is someone you have not forgiven.

_____ I can't forgive my mother. She always put me down as a child—and she still does today.

_____ I can't forgive my husband. He never has time for me and he's always criticizing me.

_____ I can't forgive my friend. She hurt me when she said words that weren't true about me—behind my back.

_____ I can't forgive my sister. She's always been my parents' favorite, and now she's taking advantage of them.

_____ I can't forgive my husband. He drinks too much and he's abusive to me and the children when he does so.

_____ I can't forgive my son (or daughter). He (or she) has been lying to us, and may even be into drugs.

_____ I can't forgive my husband. He has been accessing pornography on the Internet. That's wrong and he knows it.

_____ I can't forgive my father. He abused me as a child. If I forgave him, it would be excusing what he did.

_____ I can't forgive _____ because _____ .

All of these responses misinterpret forgiveness. To forgive someone you don't need to excuse his or her behavior. But you do need to *forgive* the person. You may have heard the adage "Hate the sin; love the sinner." It is appropriate. Perhaps your anger toward someone who has hurt you *is* justified, but you must remember the Scripture that reads, "If you do not forgive men their trespasses, neither will your Father forgive your trespasses" (Matthew 6:15). You must forgive the person if you want to be free (and forgiven!).

There are both spiritual and psychological reasons to forgive. The spiritual reason is that we desire to obey God, and He has told us to forgive others just as He has forgiven us: "And be kind to one another, tenderhearted, forgiving one another, just as God in Christ also forgave you" (Ephesians 4:32). When we forgive people who have hurt us, we restore their God-given worth and value—not because they deserve it but because God has already done the same for us.

The psychological reason to forgive others is to free ourselves from the pain and the victimization that other people have inflicted on us. When we forgive, we make a choice to no longer allow other people's sin to dictate how we feel or what we do. Forgiveness gives us the freedom to truly live our lives as God intended.

Think about someone who has injured you, someone toward whom you still feel resentment. Place this person's name in this blank _____ (or you may want to take out a piece of paper and write all of this exercise outside this workbook so you can be sure it stays private).

Now that you have this person in mind, write how he or she has offended you in the space below:

Think of your own life. Have you ever done something that might have contributed to this person's acting in this way? _____ yes _____ no

Remember God loves all people as much as He loves us. He loves the murderer, the adulterer, the alcoholic, and the child abuser. And He hates all their sins as much as He hates ours. He hates murder, drunkenness, and abuse as much as He hates pride, gossiping, and unforgiveness. We may compare our sins to other people's and say, "Mine aren't so bad," but God says they all stink. Remember, forgiveness doesn't make the other person right; it makes us free.

Often we are harmed by bitterness. In his letter to the Ephesians, the apostle Paul tells these early Christians, "Let all bitterness, wrath, anger, clamor and evil speaking be put away from you, with all malice."

God cannot bless us as He'd like to if we hold on to our bitterness. In their workbook *The Choosing to Forgive Workbook*, Drs. Les Carter and Frank Minirth walk readers through the questions they ask patients to answer when they are trying to overcome bitterness. Answer these questions below as you attempt to personalize your choice to drop bitterness:

First, be honest and ask yourself, *Why would I want to remain bitter?* (For instance, "It makes me feel powerful," or "It gives me the excuse I need to withdraw from this relationship.")

Now ask, *What would be the likely consequences of clinging to bitterness?* (For instance, "I'd be less effective in developing love relationships," or "It could become a habit that would eat away at my quality of life.")

In their years of counseling people for depression, anger, and anxiety, these two doctors say they have never encountered anyone who ultimately experienced pleasant consequences from holding on to bitterness. It is doubtful that you will find the consequences of bitterness to be good either.

Realizing that bitterness is a choice but its consequences are not desirable, you should be willing to move on to one final question, as the doctors' patients are:

Why might forgiveness be a better option than bitterness? (For instance, "I'd be choosing not to live in the past, which would free me to be more effective in my current relationships," or "I could concentrate more on qualities that I do want to have in my personality."[1])

The doctors admit that no one is duty bound to forgive, nor duty bound to cease their bitterness. No amount of coercion can make people choose otherwise. People are free to choose, the doctors admit, even if it means they might make poor choices.[2]

I did not feel *like* forgiving my mother, instead I *chose* to forgive her. I did so because God's Word says, "Forgive, and you will be forgiven" (Luke 6:37). That verse also says that we shouldn't judge if we don't want to be judged ourselves.

Are you willing to forgive _____ (the person who has harmed you)? If so, write a prayer of forgiveness below. Be sure to tell the Father that you know He has forgiven your sins and that you know He expects you to forgive this person. Then ask Him to help you be completely released from all unforgiveness.

Now put this person in God's hands. Write that prayer below.

And finally pray for that person daily for the next week. You can pray the prayer you have written above over and over again. Or you can simply say a few sentences as part of your daily prayer time.

But as you pray for this person, be aware of what Screwtape says to Wormwood about such prayers. "We have means of rendering the prayers innocuous," he says. The patient's attention can be "kept on what he regards as her [the person prayed for] sins, by which, with a little guidance from you, he can be induced to mean any of her actions which are inconvenient or irritating

123

to himself. Thus you can keep rubbing the wounds of the day a little sorer even while he is on his knees."[3]

Over the next weeks and months, test yourself on the completeness of your forgiveness. If the person is someone close to you, do you find yourself going back to that mistake over and over again, as Sarah did? When you are in a disagreement with the person, do you bring that situation up? If so, you haven't truly forgiven.

Maybe you are not able to quickly forgive the person you described in the above exercises. Sometimes the hurt is deep and needs to be worked through over a period of time. You might want to buy a copy of *The Choosing to Forgive Workbook* by Dr. Les Carter and Dr. Frank Minirth or meet with a pastor or Christian counselor. If you find this is so, resolve to make an appointment to see your pastor or a counselor.

While forgiving others is crucial, forgiveness is also needed in two other areas: forgiving yourself and forgiving God.

FORGIVING YOURSELF AND GOD

Forgiving myself? you wonder. That may sound strange to many of us, but most of us do not realize the grudges we hold against ourselves.

Forgiving Yourself

Look at the statements below and check the ones that apply to you. And add a statement if you harbor some other thoughts of disappointment with yourself:

_____ I should be a better mom. I'm often busy and therefore sometimes short with my kids.

_____ I should be a more loving wife.

_____ I should be achieving more in my career.

_____ I am halfway through my life, and I feel like a failure.

_____ I _____.

I certainly was burdened by thoughts of how much more I should be achieving or what kind of mom or wife I should have been. Yet God is the only One who is perfect. I often have to say, "Self, I forgive you for not being perfect, and I thank You, God, that You are right now making me into all that You created me to be."

Are you willing to forgive yourself? If so, write a prayer of forgiveness for yourself below. Be sure to include the fact that you know God has forgiven you of your sins. Thank Him for His unconditional love and let Him know how sorry you are for these errors. Finally ask Him to help you to erase any guilt from within you.

Do you feel forgiven? After all, God said: "Humble yourselves in the sight of the Lord, and He will lift you up" (James 4:10).

Now put yourself into God's hands, as you did the person you forgave earlier in this chapter. And pray for yourself daily in the areas where you feel you need help. List those areas below and then write a prayer to ask for specific ways the Lord can help you.

1.

2.

3.

Lord, I pray:

Forgiving God

Have you ever been angry with God for anything? Have you felt that He has let you down by not answering your prayers? If you've been mad at Him, say so. "God, I've been mad at You ever since _____."

You might want to write a letter to Him in the space below.

Or you might just want to shout out to Him as if He were sitting in the chair beside you. Don't be afraid to let your anger and emotions surface. God can take our unhappiness. Just think about the psalms where David cried out to God, often in desperation:

> Why do You stand afar off, O LORD?
> Why do You hide Yourself in times of trouble? (Psalm 10:1)

> How long, O LORD? Will You forget me forever?
> How long will You hide Your face from me? . . .
> How long will my enemy be exalted over me? (Psalm 13:1–2)

> My God, My God,
> Why have You forsaken Me?
> Why are You so far from helping Me,
> And from the words of My groaning?
> O My God, I cry in the daytime, but You do not hear;
> And in the night season, and am not silent. (Psalm 22:1–2)

David, who spent many of the psalms praising God, also spent other moments crying out to God and asking where He was when David needed Him. And this didn't alienate God from David. Instead, Scripture tells us that David was beloved of God.

You probably also recognized verse 1 from Psalm 22: "My God, My God, why have You forsaken Me?" Jesus cried these words to God as He was hanging on the cross. God, He knew, is a parent who cares about our desperation and our anger.

Once you have written your letter or cried out to God as David does in the psalms, write your forgiveness of God in a prayer below. Be sure to admit your anger with Him and then ask Him to help you see things from His perspective. Also ask Him to forgive you for holding these things against Him.

Now settle the score—with others, with yourself, and with God. Slam the book shut on these memories and look forward to a new relationship with others, with yourself, and with God in the future.

GOD'S THOUGHTS ON FORGIVENESS

Read through the Scripture passages below as you think about forgiving someone who has harmed you. Write the passages in the space below the citation so
you can refer to them as you work through the process of forgiving yourself,
others, and God.

1 Peter 3:8–9

Romans 12:19–21

Jeremiah 33:8

If God can forgive you in this way, shouldn't you also be able to forgive yourself?

Romans 8:1, 33–34

PART THREE

The Obedient Walk

CHAPTER FOURTEEN

Praying to See the Link between Obedience and Blessing

GROWING UP POOR MADE IT HARD FOR ME TO PUT ALOT OF MONEY in the collection plate when I first became a believer. I always did so, but I couldn't help thinking how much food that money could buy. Another thought made this just as difficult: *What if there is a time in my future when I again have no food?* Being able to give with a joyful heart as I trusted God to meet my needs was a hard step of obedience for me to learn. But once I did, the blessings started pouring in, and I lost my fear of starving to death.

OBEDIENCE

How many times do we ask God to give us what *we* want but we don't want to give God what *He* wants? We lack what we desire most—wholeness, peace, fulfillment, and joy—because we are not obedient to God. The Ten Commandments were not given to instill guilt, but as an umbrella of blessing and protection from the rain of evil.

We need God's laws because we don't know how to make life work without them. The Bible says, "If anyone competes in athletics, he is not crowned unless he competes according to the rules" (2 Timothy 2:5).

John told the early Christians:

> Now by this we know that we know Him, if we keep His commandments. He who says, "I know Him," and does not keep His commandments, is a liar, and the truth is not in him. But whoever keeps His word, truly the love of God is perfected in him. By this we know that we are in Him. He who says he abides in Him ought himself also to walk just as He walked. (1 John 2:3–6)

Devoted Christians have always known that obedience is essential to living the Christian life. One day Charles Spurgeon, the noted English evangelist and author of the eighteenth century, was crossing a street when he suddenly stopped. It looked as though he was praying, and he was. One of his deacons waited for him on the other side of the street and said to him, "You could have been run down by a carriage. What were you doing? It looked like you were praying."

Spurgeon replied, "I was praying."

The deacon then asked, "Was it so important?"

"Indeed it was. A cloud came between me and my Savior, and I wanted to remove it even before I got across the street."

Obedience to the Lord was of utmost importance to Spurgeon. And to Oswald Chambers, who said, "If [a person] wants insight into what Jesus Christ teaches, he can only get it by obedience . . . spiritual darkness comes because of something I do not intend to obey."[1]

God is blessed by our obedience and He in turn promises to reward us with His blessings.

THE PROMISED BLESSINGS

The more I've searched the Scriptures, the more I've found that the Bible is full of blessings for those who obey God. Read through the three promises below, inserting your name in the blanks.

- *The promise of healing.* "Make straight paths for your feet, _____, so that what is lame may not be dislocated, but rather be healed" (Hebrews 12:13).

- *The promise of living a long life in peace.* "Let your heart keep my commands, _____; for length of days and long life and peace they will add to you" (Proverbs 3:1–2).
- *The promise of God fighting our battles for us.* "Oh, that _____ would listen to Me, that _____ would walk in My ways! I would soon subdue her enemies, and turn My hand against her adversaries" (modified version of Psalm 81:13–14).

There are many more promises like these, and just as many warnings of what will *not* happen in our lives if we *don't* obey. After reading them, I felt inspired to ask God to show me exactly what I needed to be doing. He was quick to answer that prayer. *Check your heart,* He said. *Are you really willing to obey? If so, those promises are there for you—and for all My children.*

THE CHOICE IS OURS—THE POWER IS HIS

I've learned that God doesn't enforce obedience. We often wish He would because it would be easier, but He gives us the choice. I had to ask Him to teach me to be obedient out of my love for Him and my desire to serve the One who has done so much for me. It helps to understand that the Lord is on our side and the call to obedience is not to make us feel like hopeless failures if we don't do everything right.

The Bible says that Noah was given new life because he did *all* that God asked him to do (Genesis 6:22). There's that word *all* again. This word seems frightening when it comes to obedience because we know ourselves well enough to doubt we can do it all. And the truth is we can't.

J. Vernon McGee explained the passage in the Bible that says "Whosoever is born of God sinneth not" (1 John 5:18 KJV) in this way: "This means that whosoever is born of God does not *practice* sin; that is, *live* in sin."[2]

We cannot expect to live perfect lives. Ecclesiastes 7:20 says, "For there is not a just man on earth who does good and does not sin." God does not expect us to be perfect, but He does expect us to try. And He is willing to help us take steps of obedience.

In this part of the book we will look at nine basic steps that I believe are important to living in the center of God's will:

- Saying yes to God each day of our lives
- Remaining separate from the world
- Being baptized
- Having fellowship with other believers
- Knowing how to give ourselves away
- Remembering Jesus' sacrifice
- Walking in faith
- Being a witness
- Finding comfort in the center of God's will

These nine steps are a guideline, not a threat. Just take one step at a time, remembering that the power of the Holy Spirit in us enables us to obey God.

Stop now and ask God to help you to begin this walk with Him. Write a prayer in the space below, telling Him you don't want anything to separate you from His presence and His love. Ask Him to show you where you are not living in obedience and to help you to do so.

GOD'S BLESSINGS FOR THOSE WHO OBEY

As I mentioned in this chapter, the Lord promises many blessings to those who obey. Here are five of these blessings. Write the promises in the spaces below and then select one to copy onto an index card that you can carry in your purse or place on your refrigerator.

Deuteronomy 7:9

John 15:10–11

Luke 6:47 48

1 Chronicles 22:13

Psalm 91:14–16

CHAPTER FIFTEEN

Praying to Say Yes to God Each Day of Your Life

THROUGHOUT THIS BOOK I HAVE MENTIONED JOSH MCDOWELL AND his popular book *Evidence That Demands a Verdict*. McDowell became a Christian as a college student, and a preface to the updated version of this book, *The New Evidence That Demands a Verdict*, tells how Jesus changed Josh's life as he said yes to God in every area, particularly his relationship with his father, who was the town drunk.

McDowell would sometimes find his mother in the barn, lying in the manure behind the cows where his dad had beaten her with a hose until she couldn't get up. At times like this he vowed, "When I am strong enough, I'm going to kill him."

Two months before he graduated from high school, Josh walked into the house after a date to hear his mother sobbing. "Son," she said, "your father has broken my heart." She put her arms around him and pulled him close. "I have lost the will to live. All I want to do is live until you graduate, then I want to die."

And as she predicted, his mother died the Friday morning after he graduated. Josh left home to attend college only a few months after the funeral or he might have killed his father.[1]

Then Josh McDowell became a Christian and had to deal with Jesus' words: "But I tell you not to resist an evil person. But whoever slaps you on your right cheek, turn the other to him also" (Matthew 5:39). This was part of his saying yes to God each day of his life.

When you buy a house you first make a large down payment. Then to keep the house you must make a smaller payment every time it comes due. You can't change your mind and say, "I don't feel like making payments!" without serious consequences.

The same is true of our relationship with God. To make Him our permanent dwelling place, our initial down payment consists of making Him Lord over our lives, as we talked about in Chapter 6. After that, ongoing payments must be made, which means saying yes whenever God directs us to do something. They are all a part of the purchase, but one happens initially and the other is eternally ongoing, just like house payments. The difference is that the Lord will take only as much payment from us as we are willing to give Him. And we can possess only as much of what He has for us as we are willing to secure with our obedience.

Taking the initial step of making Him Lord over our lives is the same for everyone. Saying yes to God every day is an individual matter. Theologians call this *sanctification*.

The word *sanctify* (*hagiazo* in the Greek) is used twenty-eight times in the Bible. *Sanctify* is defined as "to make holy, purify."[2] The process of sanctification fulfills God's goal for our lives: to make us like His Son, Jesus Christ.

In the early days of the church all Christians were called saints. Yet the apostles' letters to the churches, particularly Paul's letter to the Corinthians, make it clear that these people sinned. In the first chapter of Paul's letter he mentions "contentions among you," which were reported to him "by those of Chloe's household" (1 Corinthians 1:11). And apparently some of the quarrels between these Christians were taken to the secular courts, because Paul later says, "But brother goes to law against brother, and that before unbelievers" (6:6). In chapter 5 Paul lists yet another sin: "It is actually reported that there is sexual immorality among you" (v. 1). Quarreling, disunity, sexual immorality—these people don't sound like saints. Instead Paul describes people who are destroying their Christian testimony.

How could these people be thought of as holy? Theologians tell us that sanctification has a positional as well as a practical aspect. All believers are set apart by the Holy Spirit as soon as they believe. We become saints. Positional sanctification is just as complete for the weakest and youngest believer as it is for the strongest and oldest. Positional sanctification depends *only upon one's union with Christ.* Paul knew all of the Corinthian Christians' sins yet he opened his letter to them with this greeting: "To the church of God which is at Corinth, to those who are sanctified in Christ Jesus" (1 Corinthians 1:2). All Christians are sanctified through our belief in Jesus, who died for our sins on the cross.

But we should also be constantly growing more holy in our lifestyle. That is *practical* or *progressive* sanctification, which occurs as we try to say yes to God each day of our lives.

Paul urged the Corinthians to join him in practical sanctification: "Let us cleanse ourselves from all filthiness of the flesh and spirit, perfecting holiness in the fear of God" (2 Corinthians 7:1). And he reminded the Corinthians: "Do you not know that your body is the temple of the Holy Spirit who is in you, whom you have from God, and you are not your own? For you were bought at a price; therefore glorify God in your body and in your spirit, which are God's" (1 Corinthians 6:19–20).

The final sanctification is *ultimate sanctification,* which is when we become completely like Christ at His coming (1 John 3:1–3; Romans 8:29, 30; Jude 1:24–25).

Sanctification is God's will for us. Paul tells the Thessalonians: "For this is the will of God, your sanctification: that you should abstain from sexual immorality; that each of you should know how to possess his own vessel in sanctification and honor" (1 Thessalonians 4:3–4). And Paul prayed that God would establish these saints' "hearts blameless in holiness" (1 Thessalonians 3:13).

The importance of being sanctified is clearly stated in Hebrews 12:14: "Pursue peace with all men, and holiness, without which no one will see the Lord."

Sanctification, saying yes to God each day of our lives, is crucial to the Christian walk. We do this by yielding our wills to His will.

YIELDING EACH DAY

As Christians we must become a yielded instrument for God's service. Paul told the Roman Christians, "And do not present your members as instruments of unrighteousness to sin, but present yourselves to God as being alive from the dead, and your members as instruments of righteousness to God. For sin shall not have dominion over you, for you are not under law but under grace" (Romans 6:13–14).

Sanctification involves both our bodies and our minds. Paul's advice to these early believers is meant for all Christians. Write your name in the blank spaces below:

> I beseech you therefore, _____, by the mercies of God, that you present your body a living sacrifice, holy, acceptable to God, which is your reasonable service. (Romans 12:1)

And Paul is telling you, just as he told the Corinthians:

> For you, _____, were bought at a price; therefore glorify God in your body and in your spirit, which are God's. (1 Corinthians 6:20)

Paul advises all of us, "And do not be conformed to this world, but be transformed by the renewing of your mind, that you may prove what is that good and acceptable and perfect will of God" (Romans 12:2). Paul makes it clear that we are responsible to God for our thoughts and our actions, which occur through a lifetime of "renewing" our minds.

In the months after Josh McDowell's conversion, God took his hatred for his father and turned it upside-down. Five months after he became a Christian, he found himself looking his dad right in the eye and saying, "Dad, I love you." He did not want to love the man, but he did. God's love had changed his heart.

A month later Josh was involved in a serious car accident, the victim of a drunk driver, and his father came to see him. Remarkably, he was sober that day. He seemed uneasy, pacing back and forth in McDowell's room. Then he blurted out, "How can you love a father like me?"

"Dad, six months ago I hated you, I despised you. But I have put my trust in Jesus Christ, received God's forgiveness, and He has changed my life. I can't explain it all, Dad. But God has taken away my hatred for you and replaced it with love."

For the next hour father and son talked about the change in Josh's life. Then his dad said, "Son, if God can do in my life what I've seen Him do in yours, then I want to give Him the opportunity."

That day McDowell's father accepted Christ as his Savior, and he only touched alcohol once after that. He got the drink as far as his lips, and that was it—after forty years of drinking! He didn't need it anymore.

Fourteen months later, Josh's dad died from complications of his alcoholism. But in that fourteen-month period, over a hundred people in the area around their tiny hometown committed their lives to Jesus Christ because of the change they saw in the town drunk.[3]

Our ultimate goal is to think as God thinks, which ensures that we will say yes to Him every day of our lives. This can only happen through prayer to God in every decision we make and through constant meditation on His Word. Sanctification also involves releasing our dreams to the Lord and being willing to obey immediately when we hear His voice.

Releasing Our Dreams

Each of us must place our desires and dreams in the hands of God so that He might free us from those that are not His will. In other words, we secure our future by releasing our dreams to God and, if need be, allowing them to die. If we've always had a certain picture of what we think we should do, we have to be willing to let the picture be destroyed. If it really is what God has for us, He will raise us up to do that and more. If it isn't, we will be frustrated as long as we cling to it.

Do you have a dream that you haven't released to God? _____ yes _____ no

If so, write it in the space below:

Now write a prayer, asking God to help you release this dream to Him.

Enter the prayer in your prayer journal at the back of this book and watch for God to act in this situation.

Quick Response

Saying yes to God also means being willing to obey *immediately* when we hear His voice, and not waiting until all else fails or we feel like it or we're at the end of ourselves.

Again, this is done a step at a time. If you can't trust God enough to say, "Anything You ask of me, I'll do," then keep working at it. I must admit that saying yes to God was difficult for me until I read God's Word. Read the Scripture below and write your name in the blank spaces I have added to the verse. Hear God speaking these words directly to you:

> When I called, _____ did not listen; then when _____ called, I would not listen. (Zechariah 7:13 NIV)

That puts it all in perspective, doesn't it? If we want God to hear our prayers, we need to listen and respond to His voice.

Stop now and write a prayer below that asks the Lord to help you continually say yes to Him.

Sanctification is a lifelong process that will not be completed until we are with Christ. Paul told the Philippians, "And I am sure that God, who began the good work within you, will continue his work until it is finally finished on that day when Christ Jesus comes back again" (Philippians 1:6 NLT).

This promise is for all of us. Read through Paul's words again, filling your name in the blank.

And I am sure that God, who began the good work within you, _____, will continue His work until it is finally finished on that day when Christ Jesus comes back again.

As you continue your walk with Christ, be assured that God will be faithful to continue His work of sanctification until you meet the Lord in heaven.

PROMISES OF FUTURE SANCTIFICATION

The third and final part of God's process of sanctification in our lives is future or final sanctification. Look up the Scripture passages that promise we will become like Christ when He returns for us and write them in the space below each passage.

1 John 3:1–3

Romans 8:29–30

Jude 24–25

Sanctification is a lifelong process, but the journey brings a peace and delight that can only come from having embraced the mind of Christ.

CHAPTER SIXTEEN

Praying to Remain Separate from the World

IN MY BOOK *PRAYING GOD'S WILL FOR YOUR LIFE*, I TOLD ABOUT hearing Dolores Hayford (Pastor Jack's mother) tell of a conversation with her youngest son, Jim. One day young Jim realized that some people have blessing upon blessing while others don't. He asked his mother, "Why do some people get all the breaks with God?"

After giving it some thought, Mrs. Hayford said, "Son, those who get the breaks with God are the ones who first break from the world."

And her advice was quite biblical. The Bible says, "Whoever therefore wants to be a friend of the world makes himself an enemy of God" (James 4:4).

Strong words. *Certainly I don't want to be an enemy of God*, I thought the day I heard Dolores Hayford speak. In the next weeks I asked myself two questions: What exactly is the "world"? And how do I break away from it?

The Greek word for *world* in the Bible is *kosmos*, which means "order" or "arrangement." One of the meanings of this Greek word is the organized system that is under the devil's control and leaves out God and Christ.[1]

In the apostle John's letter to the Gentile congregations, he says, "We know that we are of God, and the world lies under the sway of the wicked one" (1 John 5:19). Earlier in this epistle, John warns these new Christians, "Do not love the world or the things in the world. If anyone loves the world, the love of the Father is not in him. For all that is in the world—the lust of the flesh, the lust of the eyes, and the pride of life—is not of the Father but is of the world" (1 John 2:15–17).

No wonder Dolores Hayford told her son to break from the world.

Yet many of us fight the lure of materialism—a lovely home, a new car, worldly success—many days of our lives.

Scripture tells us that remaining in the world can have dire consequences for the Christian. As I mention them to you, ask yourself if you have experienced any of these consequences.

CONSEQUENCES OF A WORLDLY VIEW

We open ourselves up to four consequences when we maintain too close a relationship with the world.

1. A Tendency to Turn Away from the Lord's Work and Other Believers

Paul spent his last days in a cold Roman cell, without hope of acquittal because of a false charge of defiling the Temple by bringing a Gentile into it. In his second letter to Timothy, Paul tells his friend, "Demas has forsaken me, having loved this present world, and has departed for Thessalonica" (4:10). This Christian and others left Paul while he was in prison, abandoning him because they feared for their own lives. They were closer to the world than they were to their Lord Jesus Christ and His servant Paul. If we are not careful, we, too, can be lured by our fear of the world and its forces.

Are there moments when you have tended to turn away from the Lord's work or other Christians? If so, list them below and ask God to help you be strong in Him.

2. Alienation from God

I already quoted James's warning to the first-century Jewish Christians: "Whoever therefore wants to be a friend of the world makes himself an enemy of God" (James 4:4). To me the choice is clear: Whose side do you want to be on? The Lord's or the world's? Or think about it this way: Whom do you want on your side? The Lord or the world? It's either/or.

In *The Screwtape Letters*, Screwtape tells Wormwood how prosperity can alienate human beings from God. He says:

> If, on the other hand, the middle years prove prosperous, our position is even stronger. Prosperity knits a man to the World. He feels that he is "finding his place in it," while really it is finding its place in him. His increasing reputation, his widening circle of acquaintances, his sense of importance, the growing pressure of absorbing and agreeable work, build up in him a sense of being really at home on Earth, which is just what we want.[2]

Are there times when you have felt alienated from God? If so, list them below:

3. Temptation to Sin

The apostle Peter wrote two letters to the early church—the first, a letter of encouragement, and the second, a letter to warn Christians about false teachers and to encourage these early believers to grow in their faith. In this second letter, Peter tells them, "As His divine power has given to us all things that pertain to life and godliness through the knowledge of Him who called us by glory and virtue" (2 Peter 1:3). He goes on to say, "by which have been given to us exceedingly great and precious promises, that through these you may be partakers of the divine nature *having escaped the corruption that is in the world through lust*" (2 Peter 1:4, emphasis added).

If we get close to Jesus and stay away from a close association with the world, Jesus promises us that we will be partakers of His divine nature, which will keep us from the lust that is in the world.

Think of the last week. Are there times when you have been tempted to sin? List them at the top of the next page:

Now write a prayer asking God to break the hold that these temptations have on your life. List them below:

4. Deception by False Teachers

Throughout the New Testament we are warned about false teachers, particularly those who will arise during the end times. None of us know when the end of our world will occur, but we need to be careful about whose teaching we accept. In his letter to the Gentile congregations, the apostle John warns these early Christians, "Beloved, do not believe every spirit, but test the spirits, whether they are of God; because many false prophets have gone out into the world" (1 John 4:1). And in his second letter, John repeats this warning, "For many deceivers have gone out into the world who do not confess Jesus Christ as coming in the flesh. This is a deceiver and an antichrist" (2 John 7). Scripture tells us that if we remain too close to the world, we are likely to be deceived by these deceivers.

Are there people who might be deceiving you about your religious beliefs? If so, you need to test their words against the truth of Scripture. If the two don't align, you need to stay away from their teaching.

And how can we overcome the world's temptations? By cultivating a greater love for the Father than we have for the world. The Christian who seeks daily to please God in everything and who strives for spiritual growth through prayer, the study of God's Word, and witnessing will not fall prey to the temptations of the world.

Stop now and write a prayer, asking God to help you to overcome the temptation to be lured by the world. Be sure to ask Him to take away anything in your life that isn't of Him. And ask Him to help you to be released from longing for these things. Finally, ask Him to help you draw closer to Him each day of your life.

When I was asking myself those two questions: What exactly is the "world" and How do I break away from it, I also read another Scripture: "Be sober, be vigilant; because your adversary the devil walks about like a roaring lion, seeking whom he may devour" (1 Peter 5:8).

We cannot remain separate from the world unless we also identify the force within the world that is choosing to harm us. Before I became a Christian, I had rejected the idea of a personal devil as basically naive. Then I realized that breaking away from the world means recognizing our enemy—Satan—and refusing to be aligned with him in any way.

IDENTIFYING THE ENEMY

The role of Satan against the Christian is summed up by the meaning of his name. *Satan* means "adversary." He is also called "the devil," meaning the accuser. He can appear as a hideous dragon (Revelation 12:3–4, 9) or as a beautifully deceptive "angel of light" (2 Corinthians 11:14). To help you understand who he is, I have included a list of some of the names of Satan at the end of this chapter.

Satan's objective is to do anything he can to undermine a Christian's faith. He wages battle against us in five ways.

1. Accusing Us

Certainly the devil accused God's servant Job. "The only reason Job loves You," Satan told God, "is because You have been so good to him." Satan put Job through a series of trials—losing his health, his fortune, and his children—as a test of his love for God.

In the midst of all this suffering, Job attests, "For I know that my Redeemer lives, and He shall stand at last on the earth. And after my skin is destroyed, this I know, that in my flesh I shall see God" (Job 19:25–26). God rewarded Job for remaining separate from the world. In the end He doubled Job's material blessings—and gave him a second family of sons and daughters.

The book of Revelation tells us that Satan is also accusing us. The apostle John describes part of his vision in this way: "Then I heard a loud voice saying in heaven, 'Now salvation, and strength, and the kingdom of our God, and the power of His Christ have come, for the accuser of our brethren, who accused them before our God day and night, has been cast down" (Revelation 12:10).

Satan lives up to his name as the accuser, but in the end he will be cast into the lake of fire and brimstone (Revelation 20:10).

Satan will also attempt to destroy our testimony for Christ.

2. Destroying Our Testimony for Christ

In Peter's first letter to the Jewish believers who were being persecuted he warned them, "Be sober, be vigilant; because your adversary the devil walks about like a roaring lion seeking whom he may devour" (1 Peter 5:8).

Can you think of times in your life when you have acted in a way that does not glorify Christ? If so, list them below:

How can you keep from making these mistakes again?

Satan will accuse us, he will try to destroy our testimony for Christ, and he will attempt to deceive us.

3. Deceiving Us

Scripture identifies Satan as a deceiver (Revelation 20:10). And Paul warns the Corinthians that Satan could deceive them: "For such are false apostles, deceitful workers, transforming themselves into apostles of Christ. And no wonder! For Satan himself transforms himself into an angel of light. Therefore it is no great thing if his ministers also transform themselves into ministers of righteousness, whose end will be according to their works" (2 Corinthians 11:13–15).

"Deceiver" is certainly an accurate description for the devil. In *The Screwtape Letters*, Screwtape advises Wormwood about how to deceive the patient: "Every dictator or even demagogue—almost every film star or crooner—can now draw tens of thousands of the human sheep with him. They give themselves (what there is of them) to him; in him, to us. There may come a time when we shall have no need to bother about *individual* temptation at all, except for the few. Catch the bellwether, and his whole flock comes after him."[3]

Can you think of moments in your life when Satan has deceived you? Moments when you were tempted to copy the lifestyle or beliefs of someone you admired? Or when something looked so good, you were tempted to try it? List those moments below:

Now think of how you could overcome this temptation in the future.

4. Hindering What God Would Want Us to Do

In the apostle Paul's first letter to the Thessalonians, he tells them, "Therefore we wanted to come to you—even I, Paul, time and again—but Satan hindered us" (2:18). Paul wanted to be near these new Christians so he could nurture their faith, but he felt that the events in his current life, influenced by Satan, had kept him from returning to Thessalonica.

Have you been kept from doing things you think God would want you to do? If so, list them below:

How might you change that in the future?

5. *Tempting Us Morally*

In Paul's instructions about married life, he warned the Corinthian Christians: "Do not deprive one another except with consent for a time, that you may give yourselves to fasting and prayer; and come together again so that Satan does not tempt you because of your lack of self-control" (1 Corinthians 7:5). Obviously Paul believed that Satan would take advantage of any situation that would tempt Christians to sin.

Stop now and write a prayer that asks God to help you resist Satan's influence on your life. Be sure to ask Him to help you to recognize this enemy and to turn your heart away from the world so that you will look only to God as your source and your guide.

Now you can look toward the future with hope because God will help you to remain separate from the world.

VICTORY THROUGH THE HOLY SPIRIT

The secret of victory over the world and Satan is the power of the Holy Spirit. Paul advised the Galatian Christians: "I say then: Walk in the Spirit, and you shall not fulfill the lust of the flesh. For the flesh lusts against the Spirit, and the Spirit against the flesh; and these are contrary to one another, so that you do not do the things that you wish. But if you are led by the Spirit, you are not under the law" (Galatians 5:16–18).

Breaking from the world doesn't require you to live like a hermit for the rest of your life. But you do have to run a frequent check on your heart to make sure that you are not too attached to the world. Ask yourself these questions:

1. Do I judge myself by the world's standard for beauty, acceptability, and success? _____ yes _____ no

2. Do I depend on worldly magazines and books to tell me how to live? _____ yes _____ no

3. Am I willing to ignore certain convictions I have in order to find favor with other people? _____ yes _____ no

4. Am I drawn toward emulating the lifestyles of celebrities rather than becoming who God created *me* to be? _____ yes _____ no

5. Am I willing to compromise what I know of God's ways in order to gain something I want? _____ yes _____ no

If you said yes to any of these questions, you are cutting off the possibilities God has for your life. God asks, "Since you died with Christ to the basic principles of this world, why, as though you still belonged to it, do you submit to its rules . . . ?" (Colossians 2:20 NIV). He clearly instructs us, "Do not be conformed to this world, but be transformed by the renewing of your mind, that you may prove what is that good and acceptable and perfect will of God" (Romans 12:2).

The verse I quoted earlier, where the apostle John warns the Gentiles against loving the world, ends with this promise: "And the world is passing away, and the lust of it; but he who does the will of God abides forever" (1 John 2:17). No success can be greater than this. Not only will we live forever, but we will live with our Lord Jesus Christ in heaven. Remind yourself of this as you endeavor to remain separate from the world.

EIGHT NAMES FOR SATAN

Look up the Scriptures below that describe Satan and write them in the spaces provided. Then note how you can protect yourself from this aspect of the devil.

1. The wicked one (Matthew 13:19)

    I can protect myself by _____

2. The enemy (Matthew 13:39)

    I can protect myself by _____

3. Murderer (John 8:44)

    I can protect myself by _____

4. A liar (John 8:44)

    I can protect myself by _____

5. The tempter (1 Thessalonians 3:5)

    I can protect myself by _____

6. Apollyon (Destroyer) (Revelation 9:11)

    I can protect myself by _____

7. Adversary (1 Peter 5:8)

    I can protect myself by _____

8. The Accuser (Zechariah 3:1–4)

    I can protect myself by _____

CHAPTER SEVENTEEN

Praying to Be Baptized

A FEW YEARS AFTER MICHAEL AND I WERE BAPTIZED IN PAT BOONE'S pool, a couple visited us to ask for prayer for their marriage. The woman was suffering from depression, and we soon learned that there was a certain immorality and sin in each of their backgrounds. As we talked together I began going through the basics of obedience with them, just as we are now. I believe that we short-circuit our spiritual growth if we don't set up the right foundations in the Lord. The couple answered my inquiries easily and willingly. Yes, the husband and wife had both received the Lord; yes, they attended church together; but they hesitated when I mentioned baptism. Finally, they admitted, no, they had never been baptized.

"Why don't you consider being baptized in our pool?" I suggested.

"No," the husband said, and his wife agreed.

"Well, go to your church and say you want to be baptized there," I answered. I went on to explain why this was so important to them. "Jesus said, 'Repent and be baptized,' so I believe this is a step of obedience you need to take."

This couple refused to be baptized, and I could never figure out why. After all these years, they still have not taken this step of obedience. And they still have trouble in their marriage and tremendous difficulties with their children. I have always believed that if they had taken this step, they would have found break-through in their lives. If each of them had only said, "I want to be baptized because I want my past to be buried," maybe they wouldn't still be living their lives with one foot in the past, carrying a weight that continually stunts their spiritual growth.

At one Wednesday evening prayer meeting after I received the Lord as Savior, Pastor Jack explained that baptism isn't just a ritual or an optional meaningless tradition; it is a commandment of Jesus. "Going against a tradition that is ordained by God brings trouble, and you jeopardize your fruitfulness by ignoring it," he said. "When you come to baptism, you are turning your back on your old life. You are saying, 'Lord, You have died for me, now I am dying to myself to receive Your life.' His death on the cross sealed the covenant from His side. Your response in baptism is saying, 'Lord, I seal the covenant from my side, but it's Your power that makes it work.'"

The next day as Michael and I talked about the fact that we were limiting what God could do in us and possibly bringing trouble into our lives by not being obedient, we decided to take this step of obedience, even though we had been baptized as children.

A BABY STEP OF GIANT SIGNIFICANCE

Baptism is a very simple first step in learning to obey God, and it only has to be done once if you understand what you're doing. But if baptism had no meaning for you (either because you were a baby or had no relationship with the Lord), you need to be baptized now.

Jesus Himself was baptized in order to do what was right, and He commanded us all to do the same, saying, "He who believes and is baptized will be saved" (Mark 16:16).

Jesus considered baptism to be so important that He made it an essential part of the Great Commission, the last words He spoke to His disciples. He said, "Go therefore and make disciples of all the nations, baptizing them in the name of the Father and of the Son and of the Holy Spirit" (Matthew 28:19).

Baptism by water in the names of the three persons in the Trinity has been practiced by the church from its beginning. Even Paul, who said he was not sent to baptize (1 Corinthian 1:14–17), baptized the household of Stephanas. And Paul, Peter, and Philip ended their preaching with a call for repentance and baptism.

One such instance occurred at Pentecost, when the people who heard Peter's call for repentance asked him, "What shall we do?" He immediately responded, "Repent, and let every one of you be baptized in the name of Jesus Christ for the remission of sins; and you shall receive the gift of the Holy Spirit" (Acts 2:37–38).

As circumcision was the sign and seal of the Abrahamic covenant to the Jewish faith, so baptism is the sign and seal of the New Covenant of the Christian faith.

Throughout the ages some Christians have felt that baptism by immersion is important. J. Vernon McGee said, "Frankly, although I was reared a Presbyterian, I think that immersion is a more accurate type of this identification [in Romans 6:4]."[1]

McGee also said, "We must recognize that we have to be identified with Christ, and this is accomplished by the Holy Spirit. Our water baptism is a testimony to this. One time an old salt said to a young sailor in trying to get him to accept Christ and be baptized, 'Young man, it is *duty* or *mutiny!*' And when you come to Christ, my friend, you are to be baptized because it is a duty. If you are not, it is mutiny."[2]

The apostle Paul also emphasized the sacrament of baptism. He asked those who heard him give his testimony before he was taken to jail, "And now why are you waiting? Arise and be baptized, and wash away your sins, calling on the name of the Lord" (Acts 22:16).

Have you been baptized with water? _____ yes _____ no

Were you baptized at an age when you fully understood its significance? _____ yes _____ no

If not, you need to do so.

Before you take this step of obedience, you might want to ask yourself the questions that are a part of some baptismal services. These questions are either asked of the parents of babies or children or of the adult who is being baptized:

- Do you renounce Satan and all the spiritual forces of wickedness that rebel against God?

- Do you repent of all sinful desires that draw you from the love of God?

- Do you turn to Jesus Christ and accept Him as your Savior?

- Do you put your whole trust in His grace and love?

- Do you promise to follow and obey Him as your Lord?

Write a prayer below, asking for God's guidance in this area of obedience. If you have never been baptized, ask God to help you take this important step.

If you have already been baptized, explain below what the experience meant to you.

THE SACRAMENT OF BAPTISM

Baptism was part of the apostles' conversion of Gentiles and the Jews. Work through the passages below, which show moments of baptism in the early church. Write the passages in the blank space and then answer the questions. (In some cases you will have to read the entire chapter to understand the significance of the baptism, but you only need to write the verse or verses mentioned below in the space.)

Acts 8:12

Who was baptized?

Who baptized these people?

Why were they being baptized?

Acts 10:44–47

Who was baptized?

Who baptized these people?

Why were they being baptized?

Acts 18:8

Who was baptized?

Who baptized these people?

Why were they being baptized?

CHAPTER EIGHTEEN

Praying to Have Fellowship with Other Believers

MANY CHRISTIANS HAVE BEEN BLESSED BY THE JOY AND SPIRITUAL insights of author and artist Joni Eareckson Tada, who has been a quadriplegic since a swimming accident when she was a teenager. Joni has ministered to many people's hearts in the years since that accident, including mine. Yet throughout her years of ministry, Joni *herself* has been ministered to by other Christians. For example, eight different girls on seven different mornings each week come to her house at 7:30 A.M. to fix coffee, help exercise her legs, give her a bed bath, get her dressed, and sit her up in her wheelchair. These are women, just like you and me, the kind who stand in line in front of you at the grocery store or whom you run into at the local coffee shop. They include a seamstress, a hairstylist, a bookkeeper, a secretary, a data-entry supervisor, a mother and daughter, and an administrator. They have homes and family members, mortgage payments, and kitchen appliance problems. But they come to help Joni each week because of their Christian commitment and faith in God.[1]

MORE THAN JUST FRIENDSHIP

The word *fellowship* sounded strange and "churchy" when I first heard it, like tea and cookies after a missionary meeting or a potluck dinner in the church basement. I've since learned that it's much more than just coffee hour. *Fellowship* is defined as "companionship, a friendly association, mutual sharing, a group of people with the same interests."² In the biblical sense, it's even more than that.

Fellowship was one of the four staples of the New Testament church, along with the apostles' doctrine, prayer, and the breaking of bread (Acts 2:42).

After Pastor Jack exhorted us to "be in fellowship with other believers" and waved his hand across the congregation as if to get his sheep moving, he said. "Fellowship has to do with a mutuality in all parts of your life. You bear one another's burdens and fulfill the law of Christ. You pray for one another, you love one another, you help one another when there is material need, you weep with those who weep and rejoice with those who rejoice. It's growing in an association with people who are moving in the same pathway you are and sharing with each other in your times of victory or need or your times of trial or triumph. It's growing in relationship."

Let's look at these ideas and a few others that Scripture suggests as part of the fellowship with other believers inside the church.

Fellowship Inside the Church

Bearing One Another's Burdens

The early Christians were truly a community of believers. There are numerous instances throughout Acts and Paul's letters to the churches when Christians sent money and relief to other congregations. Here are a few examples:

- "Then the disciples, each according to his ability, determined to send relief to the brethren dwelling in Judea" (Acts 11:29).

- "But now I am going to Jerusalem to minister to the saints, for it pleased those from Macedonia and Achaia to make a certain contribution for the poor among the saints who are in Jerusalem" (Romans 15:25–26).

- "Now concerning the collection for the saints, as I have given orders to the churches of Galatia, so you must do also: On the first day of the week let each one of you lay something aside, storing up as he may prosper, that there be no collections when I come" (1 Corinthians 16:1–2).

Throughout Paul's letters to the churches he encourages this kind of ministry. When he wrote to the Roman Christians about their responsibilities to society, he mentioned, "distributing to the needs of the saints, given to hospitality" (Romans 12:13). He echoes this advice in his letter to the Jewish Christians: "But do not forget to do good and to share, for with such sacrifices God is well pleased" (Hebrews 13:16).

And in his second letter to the Corinthians he gave an example of the sacrifice the Macedonian Christians made for the impoverished believers in Jerusalem:

> Moreover, brethren, we make known to you the grace of God bestowed on the churches of Macedonia: that in a great trial of affliction the abundance of their joy and their deep poverty abounded in the riches of their liberality. For I bear witness that according to *their* ability, yes, and beyond *their* ability, *they* were freely willing, imploring us with much urgency that we would receive the gift and the fellowship of the ministering to the saints. (8:1–4)

In this example mission churches—the churches in Macedonia—are giving to the mother church, the church in Jerusalem. Christianity had begun there and then reached out to other parts of Asia through the apostles' ministry. Yet the church in Jerusalem was now weakened by persecution. In fact, there was a famine in the city, and the church was poverty-stricken. So the other churches responded. The Macedonian church, which was poor itself, even gave "beyond their ability freely"—not grudgingly. And Paul is not talking here about a tithe or regular giving to the church. He's talking about ministering to special needs.

In his commentary *Thru the Bible: 1 Corinthians through Revelation,* J. Vernon McGee says, "It is a wonderful thing to give to the missions, but must we neglect folks in our own congregations who are in need? Many of them don't even want their needs to be known in the local congregation because they know it would become a subject of gossip in the church. They don't want to accept help because they feel it would be more or less a disgrace."

Then McGee mentions how he handled such situations in his own church. "Sometimes I could not reveal the name of the person in need to a committee or a group that wanted to know to whom the help was going, because the committee would not keep it in confidence. . . . We have lost today this wonderful grace of giving."[3]

The Lord calls us to have fellowship with other believers so we can bear each other's burdens. He also calls us to be regular in our church attendance.

Regular Attendance

We cannot receive what God has in mind for us by attending church just once or twice a month. The author of Hebrews is very clear about this: "And let us consider one another in order to stir up love and good works, not forsaking the assembling of ourselves together, as is the manner of some, but exhorting one another, and so much the more as you see the Day approaching" (Hebrews 10:24–25).

Even in New Testament days some Christians neglected regular attendance at the worship services of their local church. The writer of Hebrews points out that as members of a local church we have an obligation to one another. We are to provoke one another to good works and to exhort one another to live consistent lives worthy of God. The ultimate reason that we should participate in a local church is because God specifically commands that we do so in Hebrews 10:24–25.

Finally God wants us to be in fellowship with other believers so that we will have pastoral oversight.

Pastoral Oversight

Peter wrote his letters to Jewish believers who were struggling in the midst of persecution. He ended his first letter by exhorting the elders of these churches to "shepherd the flock of God." He told them to serve as overseers, "not by constraint but willingly, not for dishonest gain but eagerly; nor as being lords over those entrusted to you, but being examples to the flock" (1 Peter 5:1–3).

Each of us needs accountability, whether it be to our minister or to other members of the church, often those within our Bible study or home group.

It's very important that we find a church home and spend time with that body of believers. And as we do so, we need to be careful about judging those who worship there. Screwtape told Wormwood that such a judgmental attitude could lead their "patient" astray:

> When he gets to his pew and looks round him he sees just that selection of his neighbours whom he has hitherto avoided . . . It matters very little, of course, what kind of people that next pew really contains. You may know

one of them to be a great warrior on the Enemy's side. No matter. Your patient, thanks to Our Father Below, is a fool. Provided that any of those neighbours sing out of tune, or have boots that squeak, or double chins, or odd clothes, the patient will quite easily believe that their religion must therefore be somehow ridiculous.[4]

People who are truly committed to the Lord approach church with a far different attitude, one which Rich Mullins's biographer, James Bryan Smith, learned from Mullins: "Because of Rich I go to church with a different perspective. I value the people around me more because I see how much I need them, and I am less concerned with how it all looks and sounds. Rich often said that he loved to go to church because 'It's the only place where men will sing, and the only place where people aren't afraid to do something they do so badly so loudly.' The point is not about aesthetics or performance or even being contemporary. It is about connecting myself to the body of Christ and participating in the praises of His people."[5]

How do you evaluate a church? My checklist includes the following:

- The pastor believes the Bible is the Word of God and offers good, solid teaching from it.

- You sense the love of God there and receive it abundantly from the people.

- The pastor talks about the Holy Spirit's power in a Christian's life.

- The members of the congregation praise and worship the Lord.

Ask God to lead you to the right place if you aren't already a member of a church. When you find it, make a commitment to stay and watch yourself grow. There is also strength in being with believers outside the church.

OUTSIDE THE CHURCH

Relationships with Christians

When you make friends with people who follow the Lord, there is a strong bond of love that makes other relationships seem shallow. Such friendships are the most fulfilling and healing. They can also be the most frustrating because we expect *Christians* to be perfect when in reality only *Christ* is perfect.

It's helpful to think of all fellowship with believers as beneficial: The pleasant encounters are *healing* and the unpleasant ones are stretching. When you run across believers who stretch you more than you feel you can handle, don't turn away from God. He always loves and respects you, even if a few of His offspring don't. We need to be merciful to those who "stretch" us, and forgive quickly. Besides we are probably stretching others ourselves.

Is a fellow Christian "stretching" you right now? _____ yes _____ no

If so, how can you forgive this person? By trying to understand what is driving him or her to do what he or she is doing? By remembering that only Christ is perfect? Ask God to show you ways you are "stretching" others around you.

Relationships with Non-Christians

The Bible says we should "not be unequally yoked together with unbelievers" (2 Corinthians 6:14), but this doesn't mean that we should avoid them. It just means that our closest relationships, the ones that deeply touch and guide our lives, need to be with believers.

Ask yourself, "Am I a godly influence in the lives of my unbelieving friends?" If so, then consider the relationship good.

If, however, they influence you away from God and His ways, then cut off the relationships immediately. Screwtape is overjoyed when he learns that Wormwood's "patient" has made some new acquaintances. He says:

> I gather that the middle-aged married couple who called at his office are just the sort of people we want him to know—rich, smart, superficially intellectual, and rightly skeptical about everything in the world . . .
>
> No doubt he must very soon realize that his own faith is in direct opposition to the assumptions on which all the conversation of his new friends is based . . . If he is a big enough fool you can get him to realize the character of the friends only while they are absent; their presence can be made to sweep away all criticism. If this succeeds, he can be induced to live, as I have known many humans live, for quite long periods, two parallel lives; he will not only appear to be, but will actually be, a different man in each of the circles he frequents.[6]

If the unbelievers influence you in these ways, sever the relationship at once. You should also stop the relationship if the friendship does not seem to be beneficial.

Christians and Non-Christians

We will ultimately be let down or disappointed if our first goal in any relationship is our own fulfillment. As painful as it is, we have to give up that desire and lay it at Jesus' feet. However, there may be times when we have done all we can do in a relationship and it is still filled with problems. As hard as we try to make things good, a certain person may always leave us feeling depressed, angry, insecure, frightened, or hurt. When that happens, it is best to let the friendship go and give it to God to restore or remove as He sees fit.

Fellowship is a step of obedience that expands our hearts, bridges gaps, and breaks down walls. It encourages, fulfills, and balances our lives. All of this is necessary for spiritual well-being and a fruitful life in the will of God.

Write a prayer below, asking the Lord to lead you to the people He wants you to know, people who will help you grow in Him or people whom you can lead to Him.

BENEFITS OF PARTICIPATING IN THE LOCAL CHURCH

Scripture lists many benefits of participating in a local church. Write the particular passage below the Scripture verses; then list the benefit.

Acts 20:7

The benefit here is _____.

Matthew 18:15–17 or 2 Corinthians 13:1–10

The benefit in this passage is _____.

1 Peter 5:1–3

The benefit in this passage is _____.

Acts 2:42–47

Seven benefits for participation are listed in this passage of Scripture. They are:

CHAPTER NINETEEN

Praying to Know How to Give Yourself Away

I USED TO THINK I WAS A GENEROUS PERSON. THAT IS, UNTIL I MET Patti. I was introduced to her when I did a radio interview for a Christian organization where she worked part-time. She was gracious, helpful, supportive, and put me at ease immediately. It was impossible not to love her. As we talked briefly after the program, we discovered we attended the same church and our daughters were the same age. Yet in a congregation of twelve thousand with multiple church services, our paths had never crossed.

I saw more of Patti after our young daughters began to attend the same elementary school. We would wave to one another in the parking lot or call out greetings in the schoolyard, but I didn't really get to know her until after I had major surgery.

A number of wonderful women at the church had arranged to bring food to our family every night for three weeks after I returned home from the hospital. I had never experienced that kind of care before, and I was touched by it. My young children would surely have starved, or we would have eaten pizza every night for three weeks, if it weren't for the sacrifices of these thoughtful ladies.

After the fifth night, I received a call from Patti, who was to deliver dinner.

"I need to come over early, if that's all right with you," she said. "I have a lot of things to unload."

"You do? What kind of dinner is this?" I asked.

"Oh, it's not one dinner, it's five," she answered in a way that let me know she didn't think this was out of the ordinary. "And I have some things to occupy your time while you're recovering."

"Come whenever is convenient for you," I said. "I'm definitely not going anywhere in the near future."

"I'll be there at two this afternoon."

That was a full three hours before any of the other women arrived. I wondered if it was going to take that long to unload her car.

When my doorbell rang at 2:00 P.M., I hobbled slowly to the front door. Patti's arms were filled with a stack of freezer cartons, so I pointed her toward the kitchen.

"What have you done, Patti?" I exclaimed. "How much food have you brought?"

"Oh, this is just the beginning," she said with a laugh. "This isn't even all of the first meal."

I glanced at her car and couldn't believe what I saw. It was filled with freezer cartons and cardboard boxes piled high.

"Patti, this isn't *all* for me, is it?" I said, certain she would say no.

"Oh, yes, it is. It's everything a person needs to get well," she replied over her shoulder as she headed toward the kitchen.

I apologized for being unable to help her carry anything in and called my husband, who was working in the studio off the garage, to come and assist her. It must have taken him ten trips to her car before everything was inside. He was as amazed as I was to see what she had done.

"All the elements of each dinner go together, and they are number coded," she explained after everything was stacked in the kitchen. "For example, dinner number one has a chicken dish, a vegetable dish, a potato dish, homemade bread, and a dessert. So these five cartons with the number one on them all go together."

"Homemade bread?" I repeated in astonishment. "You made homemade bread?"

"Oh, yes, and here is the jam to go with it," she said as she searched one of the boxes.

"Oh, good!" I sighed. "I was so worried you might have forgotten something."

She laughed confidently. "Number two is the lamb dinner, and here are the vegetables that go with it, and this is the rice dish. That container holds the blackberry cobbler, and here are the homemade rolls."

"Homemade rolls? You actually prepared homemade rolls? And homemade blackberry cobbler?"

She laughed again and continued on and on until she had explained each dinner.

On the labels of each freezer container I noticed she had written instructions for the oven's temperature, how long the food should cook, which container to put in the oven first, and when to put the others in so everything would be synchronized.

After she had put the food away, she started to unpack the boxes but stopped and said, "Let me take all this into your bedroom. That's probably where you'll be using these things."

Slowly I led the way into our bedroom.

"These are my favorite magazines, books, and videos," she said of the stacks that she began laying neatly next to my night table. "Each one is uplifting, and I know you'll love them. Here is some body lotion and Chap Stick. I know how dry your skin can get after surgery. And these are great tapes of worship songs and a few of my favorite teachings on the Bible. I also brought a tape recorder in case you didn't have one small enough to fit on your nightstand." She went on to give a detailed explanation of every item.

When she was done, I laughed, even though it hurt to do so. "I don't believe you, Patti. How in the world did you ever find time to do all this? Are you Superwoman or an angel?"

"Oh, I just prepared an especially nice meal for my family every night for the past five nights, and doubled the portions so I could freeze half for you. As for the rest of it, I simply went through my house and gathered all the things I love and thought you might enjoy."

"I'm overwhelmed. How can I ever repay you or thank you for all you've done?"

"Seeing your joy is reward enough for me," she said and then hugged me goodbye.

Over the next few days we ate every wonderful bite of the food she had made.

Over the next few weeks, I enjoyed all the items she had brought. Over the next few months, Patti and I became the best of friends, and so did our daughters.

But the most amazing part of this story is that was only the beginning. Patti's generosity hasn't decreased in all these years. She has taught me what friendship and sacrificial giving truly mean, and I'm still her student to this day.

Patti's desire to give comes both from her natural inclination to help others and from her knowledge of God's Word.

THE WORD OF THE LORD ON GIVING

When I heard Pastor Jack preach on giving I realized that giving is actually giving *back* to God from what He has given us. Giving is a step of obedience that brings life, health, healing, and abundance. The Bible says that a person who gives will have a secure heart and will triumph over his foes. Two types of giving are important: giving to the Lord and giving as unto the Lord.

Giving to the Lord

Seven hundred Scriptures in the Bible deal with money. That's because the first and greatest commandment is "Thou shalt love the Lord thy God with all thy heart, and with all thy soul, and with all thy mind" (Matthew 22:37 KJV). And the first commandment of the Ten Commandments given to Moses in the wilderness was "Thou shalt have no other gods before me" (Exodus 20:3 KJV).

Unfortunately most of us tend to be lured by a god called materialism. Counselors often tell me that they ask a counselee to look at his or her checkbook. "Where are you spending your money?" they ask. The answer to this question tells a great deal about a person since the old adage "Where your money is, there is your heart also" is so true.

God calls us to tithe 10 percent of our increase, and He does so in very strong words. Read through His message to the Israelites in Malachi 3:8–10:

> "Will a man rob God?
> Yet you have robbed Me!
> But you say,
> 'In what way have we robbed You?'
> In tithes and offerings.

You are cursed with a curse,
For you have robbed Me,
Even this whole nation.
Bring all the tithes into the storehouse,
That there may be food in My house,
And prove Me now in this,"
Says the LORD of Hosts.
"If I will not open for you the windows of heaven
And pour out for you such blessing
That there will not be room enough to receive it."

This is not a new commandment from the Lord; the tithing system began during the time of Moses. Giving reminds us that everything we have comes from the Lord. And this passage in Malachi is the only place in the Bible where God says, "Just test Me." And note the promise that accompanies this challenge: "I will . . . pour out for you such blessing that there will not be room enough to receive it."

A friend of mine's husband recently retired. For years she and her husband had disagreed about tithing. Slowly they had progressed from about forty dollars a week to giving 10 percent of their earnings *after* taxes. But they had never made the full commitment.

Because she was still working—and he was retired but doing a little work as an agent for a distribution company—they agreed that they would tithe in 2001. During that year God fulfilled His promise to "pour out for you such blessing." First, as part of her husband's work for this distribution company, he called the State of South Carolina to see if they had a listing of plastics companies within the state. As they talked, the man in charge mentioned that the state was interested in developing this industry in South Carolina. They exchanged thoughts about how this might happen, and after a couple of discussions between them her husband was hired as a consultant for the state.

But the major change occurred in the spring of 2001 when the plastics company he had worked for asked him to come aboard as a manufacturer's representative. They gave him accounts that had lagged since his retirement, thinking that he could baby-sit them, thus reducing the load for in-house personnel. As he began to call these accounts, he realized that one of them had recently

175

acquired a contract to produce fiber-optic cables for Australia. With work from my friend's husband this account blossomed into a very lucrative business for this company—and for my friend's husband.

In the year 2001, this man made more money in retirement than he had made as a full-time employee. My friend has kidded him, "Just think how much money you could have made if we had tithed years ago."

God fulfilled His promise to multiply His blessings to them if they tithed. But as much as they have enjoyed the increase, they did not decide to tithe to get more money; they decided to tithe out of obedience to the Lord.

Does tithing come easy for you? If not, write out a prayer below, asking God to help you move into this important area of obedience.

Giving as Unto the Lord

Besides giving *to* the Lord, we need to get into the habit of giving to others as *unto the Lord*. This means we are to bless others because it blesses God—without expecting something in return. What-will-I-get-back thinking sets us up for disappointment and unhappiness, but when we give and expect nothing in return, the Lord rewards us: "Give, and it will be given to you: good measure, pressed down, shaken together, and running over will be put into your bosom. For with the same measure that you use, it will be measured back to you" (Luke 6:38).

You saw how my friend Patti gave to me when I needed help. She obviously has a natural gift for hospitality. Most often when we give to others we do so from the gifts the Lord has gifted to us. One of the reasons He gave them to us is so they can be given away. The apostle Paul told the Ephesian Christians, "For we are His workmanship, created in Christ Jesus for good works, which God prepared beforehand that we should walk in them" (Ephesians 2:10).

Take a moment now to examine your own life.

List your particular God-given gifts on the next page. And don't be shy. He didn't give them to you for you to deny them. He sent these attributes your way for you to acknowledge them—and use them.

1. _____
2. _____
3. _____
4. _____
5. _____

Is there someone whom God would want you to minister to, using these gifts? List persons who might benefit from your reaching out to them. (For instance, if you have the gift of prayer, would this person appreciate your prayers—and a note or phone call telling him or her that you are praying?)

1. _____
2. _____
3. _____
4. _____
5. _____

Before you go further, however, you need to take stock of your time by looking at the priorities that govern your life. I hear the Bible telling us that God is first. Our families are second. Then we can become involved in church activities and ministering to others.

God's first call on us is a relationship with Him. We are not supposed to forfeit Bible study and quiet time with Him to rush about the community doing for others. I know of a woman who was highly admired in her church. She could always be counted on to support important church projects. She looked like the epitome of a Christian mother and wife when she sat in the pews on Sunday morning with her five children and her husband.

But behind that image, the counselor knew the woman was neglecting her children, and her husband was actually the homemaker in the house—and not very happy about it. When her husband tried to tell her how wrong this was, the woman accused him of sabotaging her work for the Lord.

This situation changed drastically when her eleven-year-old daughter developed cancer. Now this woman was forced to spend time at home to care for this child. At first she was angry with God because she couldn't continue her "church things."

But through introspection and counseling she realized that she had grown up in a home where both parents were achievement oriented, and that is why her church achievements had been critical to her. Fortunately the daughter recovered, and this woman's perspective changed. While there is nothing wrong with a healthy commitment to the church, this work should not be done to escape past pain or at the expense of family.

How about you? Look at your weekly schedule. How do you spend your time? Estimate the number of hours or minutes beside the specific activity.

In prayer and Bible study _____
In significant time with your husband _____
In one-on-one time with your children _____
In church-related activity _____
In household maintenance _____
In a profession away from home _____

Now ask yourself, "Is there time for a ministry to others?" _____ yes
_____ no
If so, how much? _____

Now look back at your list of God-given gifts. Which one is compatible with the time that you have available? _____

Finally look at the persons you listed who might benefit from your help. Which one needs the gift that you have selected? _____

Your gift does not have to be as extensive or elaborate as Patti's was after my surgery. Few of us can do that. Your gift might be just one meal. Or your gift might be taking a friend's child with your children to a movie or the zoo. That way you are serving your own children at the same time that you are helping a friend who might need some time to herself.

Write a prayer in the space at the top of the next page, asking God to help you reach out to the person you have selected, and pray this prayer throughout the coming week.

In *Praying God's Will for Your Life* I tell about my relationship with my friend Diane. Our gift to each other was to spend some time on the phone each week, talking about our lives and praying for each other. Whenever my life seems to be stalled, deliberately giving of myself always brings breakthrough. It's not a matter of giving to get, but of taking this step of obedience to release the flow of all God has for you. Never expect repayment. This is your service to the Lord. Sometimes you may not even want the person to know who has given the gift.

SCRIPTURAL ENCOURAGEMENT TO GIVE YOURSELF AWAY

As you consider how you might "give yourself away" in the next weeks, read through the Scripture passages below and write them in the space provided. Then consider what the Lord might be saying to you about giving to Him and His people.

1 John 3:17–19

Proverbs 3:9

Luke 6:38

Hebrews 13:16

CHAPTER TWENTY

Praying to Be Reminded of Jesus' Sacrifice

I DO A LOT OF TRAVELING AS I SPEAK THROUGHOUT THE UNITED States. I am always blessed when I'm in a church far from home and we sing the familiar songs we sing in my home church. And when we take communion together, I am very aware that my Christian brothers and sisters all over the country are sharing this same experience. We may be from different traditions and have different types of services, but we all partake of communion with the same significance. That makes each church seem like home.

I've been in communion services that were so deeply touching I was moved to tears as I thought of how Jesus was broken for me. I was reminded of how astounding it is that He not only forgave me of my sins, but He bore the consequences of them so I wouldn't have to. Because of His death on the cross, I can receive His wholeness.

Two aspects of the Communion service at the Church on the Way impressed me. First, it was called the Lord's Table. It was considered His table, not ours. It was He who invited us, not the church. Second, Communion was a joyful celebration of what Jesus accomplished for us on the cross as opposed to a mournful commemoration of His suffering. Pastor Jack called it "a celebration of victory, a reminder of Jesus' complete victory over our adversary, the enemy."

Pastor Jack's words resounded in my soul when he explained, "What Jesus says about the Lord's Table is 'I was broken for you, I bled and died for you, and I want you to never forget the deliverance and the victory and the triumph that it's intended to give you all the time. Because I did that, you don't have to be bound up in suffering and agony and hellishness. I want you to partake of that regularly and make it, every time, an annunciation of My triumph so that you're reminded of it.'"

A Joyful Reminder

Communion is a step of obedience to Jesus, who said, "Do this in remembrance of Me" (Luke 22:19). If there were no other reason, that would be enough. But it also serves to remind us that Jesus forgives, heals, and delivers, and that no power of sin, sickness, or Satan can prevail among those who lift up the power of Jesus' death in Communion. We partake of the Lord's Table to acknowledge joyfully what He accomplished for us personally on the cross so it will become a part of us. God knows we have short memories and need to be reminded frequently.

Rich Mullins saw Communion as a very personal reminder of Christ's sacrifice for him. He said: "When I go to church . . . I involve myself in something that identifies me with Augustine, that identifies me with Christ, that identifies me with nearly 2,000 years of people who have come together once a week and said, 'Let's go to the Lord's table and enjoy the feast that He has prepared for us.' In that week I may have been subjected to a million billboards that try to make me identify with the thinking of contemporary society. But once a week I go back to church and acknowledge that, though the shape of the world is really different now than it used to be, this remains the same: I still come to the Lord's table and say, 'Oh God, if it weren't for Your grace, if it weren't for the sacrifice of Christ, my life would have no meaning, no life would have real substance.' And I do that voluntarily."[1]

The Lord instituted Communion at the Last Supper, which was a celebration of the Passover Feast. During this feast the Jews traditionally passed the cup seven times; after the fourth cup they recited or sang the Hallel Psalms, Psalms 115–118. Some theologians believe that Jesus did not drink the seventh cup, but at that moment instituted the Lord's Supper. Scripture describes it this way:

And as they were eating, Jesus took bread, blessed it and broke it, and gave it to the disciples and said, "Take, eat; this is My body."

Then He took the cup, and gave thanks, and gave it to them, saying, "Drink from it, all of you.

"For this is My blood of the new covenant, which is shed for many for the remission of sins.

"But I say to you, I will not drink of this fruit of the vine from now on until that day when I drink it new with you in My Father's kingdom." (Matthew 26:26–29)

J. Vernon McGee saw Communion as representing three different moments in time: past, present, and future.

It is a commemoration. He repeats, "This do . . . in remembrance of me." This table looks back over nineteen hundred years to His death upon the cross. He says, "Don't forget that. It is important." That is to the past.

This table is a communion (sometimes we call it a communion service). It speaks of the present, of the fact that today there is a *living* Christ, my beloved.

It is a commitment. It looks to the future—that He is coming again. This table won't last forever; it is temporary. After the service it is removed, and we may not celebrate it again because we just do it until He comes. It speaks of an absent Lord who is coming back. It looks to the future.[2]

McGee also saw the future predicted in 1 Corinthians 11:26 where Paul reminds the Corinthians about Christ's words at the Last Supper, and then adds, "For as often as you eat this bread and drink this cup, you proclaim the Lord's death till He comes."[3]

EARLY OBSERVANCES OF COMMUNION

Communion was one of the four staples of the New Testament church, along with the apostles' doctrine, prayer, and fellowship. The practices of the early church are described in Acts 2, verses 42–43: "And they continued steadfastly in the apostles' doctrine and fellowship, in the breaking of bread, and in prayers. Then fear came upon every soul, and many wonders and signs were done through the apostles."

The Lord's Supper was a daily occurrence for the early Christians. Often they ate dinner together before they took Communion. And the result of the practices Paul describes? Many wonders and signs were done through the apostles. Communion is an important part of every Christian's life. It's good to take Communion regularly—at least once a month if possible, or as often as the Lord prompts you.

As you do so, you might think about inserting yourself in the following two passages from the Bible: the first, Mark 14:32–41, and the second, Matthew 28:1–7.

Two Personal Encounters with Jesus

The First Passage (Mark 14:32–41), Your First Encounter

Imagine that you are present with Jesus and His disciples in the Garden of Gethsemane. I am going to repeat this passage below, modifying it somewhat and inserting blanks for you to write your name.

> And they came to an olive grove called Gethsemane, and Jesus said, "Sit here while I go and pray." He took Peter, James, and John, and _____ with him, and he began to be filled with horror and deep distress. He told them, "My soul is crushed with grief to the point of death. Stay here and watch with me."
>
> He went on a little farther and fell face down on the ground. He prayed that, if it were possible, the awful hour awaiting him might pass him by. "Abba, Father," he said, "everything is possible for you. Please take this cup of suffering away from me. Yet I want your will, not mine."
>
> Then he returned and found the disciples and _____ asleep. "_____!" he said to _____. "Are you asleep? Couldn't you stay awake and watch with me even one hour? Keep alert and pray. Otherwise temptation will overpower you. For though the spirit is willing enough, the body is weak."
>
> Then Jesus left them again and prayed, repeating his pleadings. Again he returned to them and found [the disciples] and _____ sleeping, for they just couldn't keep their eyes open. And they didn't know what to say.

184

When he returned to them the third time, he said, "Still sleeping? Still resting? Enough! The time has come. I, the Son of Man, am betrayed into the hands of sinners. Up, let's be going. See, my betrayer is here!" (NLT)

At Communion we are often reminded of Jesus' crucifixion, but this passage shows that Jesus knew the pain He would face to erase our sins, and He dreaded it. Luke 22:44 describes Jesus' praying in the garden in this way: "And being in agony, He prayed more earnestly. And His sweat became like great drops of blood falling down to the ground." It was probably as painful for Him as He thought about Golgotha and the cross as it was for Him the day He was crucified there.

Yet He did all this for you and me. Think about that the next time you take Communion. Do you feel the blessing God has given you by forgiving your sins? If not, ask yourself why.

Early in some Communion services the minister or pastor and the people say a prayer of confession together. Then the pastor may also say these words from Matthew 5: "If you bring your gift to the altar, and there remember that your brother has something against you, leave your gift there before the altar and go your way. First be reconciled to your brother, and then come and offer your gift" (Matthew 5:23–24).

A friend of mine heard a minister recite these words in a Communion service and felt convicted. She had been quarreling with her next-door neighbor. Her "brother" definitely had something against her; she had not loved her neighbor as herself.

Although my friend felt that the quarrel had been the neighbor's fault, she knew she was not without blame. After all, it takes two to fight.

She did not take Communion that Sunday morning. And during the next week her conscience continued to tell her she must apologize. As the next Sunday drew near, she knew she had to do this before the next Communion service. She couldn't take communion with a good conscience, so she went over to her neighbor's house and said she was sorry.

My friend does not remember the conversation that day; neither does she remember what they were arguing about. She does remember that a year later when her husband was transferred out of that city, this next-door neighbor said that she had to have the going-away coffee for her. This woman told another woman who was also offering that this was very important to her—because of the mending of their friendship.

If you do not feel the Lord's presence at Communion, ask yourself the questions below:

- Have I sinned against God in thought, word, or deed?
  Write that instance here:

- Have I not done something I should have done?
  Write that instance here:

- Have I loved the Lord with my whole heart?
  If not, write that instance here:

- Have I loved my neighbor as myself?
  If not, write that instance here:

Confess these things to God by writing a prayer in the space below:

You might want to use these four questions in your daily prayer time as you confess your sins to the Father. Knowing that He forgives you should bring you joy and peace.

Finally, allow yourself to celebrate Jesus' victory as Pastor Hayford suggests. Let's consider together the second Bible passage, which is found in Matthew 28:1–7.

The Second Passage (Matthew 28:1–7), Your Second Encounter

Imagine that you are with Mary Magdalene when she went to Jesus' tomb on that Sunday morning. Again I am going to repeat this passage below, modifying it somewhat and including blanks for you to insert your name.

> Early on Sunday morning, as the new day was dawning, Mary Magdalene, and the other Mary, and _____ went out to see the tomb. Suddenly there was a great earthquake, because an angel of the Lord came down from heaven and rolled aside the stone and sat on it. His face shone like lightning, and his clothing was as white as snow. The guards shook with fear when they saw him, and they fell into a dead faint.
>
> Then the angel spoke to [Mary Magdalene, the other Mary,] and _____. "Don't be afraid!" he said. "I know you are looking for Jesus, who was crucified. He isn't here! He has been raised from the dead, just as he said would happen. Come, see where his body was lying. And now, go quickly and tell his disciples he has been raised from the dead, and he is going ahead of you to Galilee. You will see him there. Remember, I have told you, _____." (NLT)

This passage is for all of us. Christ was crucified for all of us, He rose from the dead for all of us, and we will all see Him in the future—when we are with Him in heaven.

COMMUNION AND THE LAST SUPPER

The Last Supper, during which the Lord instituted Communion, is described in three books of the Bible: Matthew, Mark, and Luke. Read the passage below and notice any differences between it and the passages in Mark and Luke:

> And as they were eating, Jesus took bread, blessed it and broke it, and gave it to the disciples and said, "Take, eat; this is My body."
>
> Then He took the cup, and gave thanks, and gave it to them, saying, "Drink from it, all of you.
>
> "For this is My blood of the new covenant, which is shed for many for the remission of sins.
>
> "But I say to you, I will not drink of this fruit of the vine from now on until that day when I drink it new with you in My Father's kingdom." (Matthew 26:26–29)

Mark 14:22–25

Luke 22:19

CHAPTER TWENTY-ONE

Praying to Be Able to Walk in Faith

IN THE YEARS AFTER I BECAME A CHRISTIAN, I REMEMBER BEING afraid that God wasn't going to come through for me when I needed help. I would say, *God, how can I know that everything is going to be okay? Why do I have so much trouble trusting these promises in Your Word?* And in my thoughts I heard God reply, *Because your father let you down and you've never really forgiven him for that.*

I was surprised at God's response I thought I had forgiven my father for not intervening when my mother punished me in such vicious ways. But God was right! I subconsciously thought that because my dad hadn't helped me the Lord probably wouldn't help me either.

After this revelation I confessed my doubt as sin, and I was set free to trust God more fully. My faith in God's ability to take care of me began to grow.

FAITH, A KEY TO LIVING THE CHRISTIAN LIFE

What is faith? The best definition of faith is in Hebrews 11:1: "Now faith is the substance of things hoped for, the evidence of things not seen." This chapter begins with the roll call of those who lived successfully by faith: people like

Noah, Abraham, Isaac, Jacob, Joseph, Moses, and Joshua. Yet as you read through the list in this forty-verse chapter, you realize that some of these people had moments when they slipped in their devotion to God.

For instance, Jacob stole his brother's birthright as the firstborn, first by coaxing Esau into "selling" it to Jacob when Esau was tired and very hungry. Essentially Esau thought, *I'm about to die of hunger. My birthright will do me no good if I'm dead, so I'll let him have it.* Then Jacob went through a masquerade with his mother, Rebekah, in which he pretended to be his brother so that his blind father would give him the firstborn's blessing.

Samson is included in this list, and he certainly made a few mistakes. The most notable one is his telling Delilah the secret of his unusual strength, which had been used to free Israel from its Philistine rulers. Since Samson was a Nazirite, he had vowed never to cut his hair; if he did so and broke this vow his God-given strength would leave him. Delilah turned this secret over to the Philistines, who shaved his hair while he slept, then poked out his eyes and made him work in a prison.

But Samson redeemed himself. Once his hair grew back, he seized an opportunity to destroy his enemy during a pagan feast. The Philistines had Samson there to exhibit him for their amusement; they didn't realize that his strength had returned until he pulled down the two major pillars that supported the building. As the walls and ceiling fell, thousands of Philistines were killed—and so was Samson.

Despite their weaknesses all of the people in this list continually fought to have the faith to give God glory. I'm sure that faith is the key to living the Christian life. In Hebrews 11:6, the writer says, "But without faith it is impossible to please Him, for he who comes to God must believe that He is, and that He is a rewarder of those who diligently seek Him."

That statement couldn't be any clearer: Without faith it is impossible to please God. If He is truly my Father and the center of my being, then I desire His love and His pleasure more than anything else in the world.

Why then is it so difficult to have faith?

WAVERING FAITH

Read through the reasons that we sometimes doubt and then apply them to your own life. Could your faith be wavering because of one of these reasons?

Times of Suffering

We may doubt God when we experience economic problems, sickness, a national calamity like September 11, 2001, or apparently unanswered prayer. Yet the person of faith believes God even when circumstances appear to the contrary.

And God is blessed by our perseverance during these times. In *The Screwtape Letters* Screwtape tells Wormwood:

> He [God, or in these letters, the Enemy] wants them to learn to walk and must therefore take away His hand; and if only the will to walk is really there He is pleased even with their stumbles. Do not be deceived, Wormwood. Our cause is never more in danger than when a human, no longer desiring, but still intending, to do our Enemy's will, looks round upon a universe from which every trace of Him seems to have vanished, and asks why he has been forsaken, and still obeys.[1]

Have you doubted God at times when you were suffering? _____ yes _____ no
    If so, describe one of those times below:

In the end did you realize that God was really there for you? _____ yes _____ no

Moments When We Are Still Immature

Paul explains that when Christians doubt sound doctrine, it is because they do not have a good enough knowledge of the Word of God and therefore are easily deceived. He says that the purpose of pastors and teachers is "for the equipping of the saints for the work of ministry . . . till we all come to the unity of the faith and the knowledge of the Son of God . . . that we should no longer be children, tossed to and fro and carried about with every wind of doctrine, by the trickery of men, in the cunning craftiness by which they lie in wait to deceive" (Ephesians 4:12–14).

About two years after I accepted Christ as Savior, I found myself doubting. *What if this Jesus thing is all a hoax?* I wondered. Yet as I worked through this thought, I realized how my life had changed since I met Him. Weighing the quality of my life before I met Jesus against the quality of my life since then, I choose to believe Him. And this little scenario happened five or six times in the first ten years of my walk with the Lord.

Do you feel that your lack of faith could be due to your either being deceived or not having a good enough knowledge of the Word of God? _____ yes _____ no

If so, check an action you might take to remedy this:

_____ Join a Bible study.

_____ Determine to attend more than one service a week.

_____ Try to read through the Bible in the next year using the Bible-reading plan in the appendix, which is taken from *The New Open Bible.*

Faith is first a decision, then an exercise in obedience, then a gift from God as it is multiplied. Our first step of faith is taken when we decide we will receive Jesus. After that, every time we decide to trust the Lord for anything, we build that faith. And whenever we decide *not* to trust Him, we tear it down. Faith is our daily decision to trust God.

Faith is obedience. Doubt is disobedience. So how can we choose to have faith each day?

FIVE STEPS TOWARD FAITH

When we are tempted to doubt, we can remedy our weakness by taking five steps toward faith:

1. Confess the doubt to God as sin.
Doubt is basically unbelief in God and His Word and is therefore sin. Paul tells the Roman Christians, "For whatever is not from faith is sin" (Romans 14:23).

We need to be totally open and honest about any doubt in God's ability or His faithfulness to provide for our every need. I've heard plenty of people say, "I told God, 'If You're out there—if You really exist—show me,'" and God answered that prayer. They admitted their unbelief.

People also admitted their unbelief to Jesus and He responded positively. For instance, a father approached the Lord and asked Him to heal his son who had seizures. And Jesus told him, "If you can believe, all things are possible to him who believes."

This father was totally honest with the Lord. He said, "Lord, I believe; help my unbelief!" (Mark 9:24).

And what did Jesus do? He healed the man's son.

2. Study the evidence for the Christian faith.

There is much evidence for the validity of Christianity, which Josh McDowell, who was at the time a prelaw student, found out when some students challenged him to intellectually examine the claim that Jesus Christ is God's Son. His research during that time and afterward can be found in his popular book *The New Evidence That Demands a Verdict*. This book of 760 pages extensively answers three questions: Is the Bible historically reliable? Is there credible evidence of Christ's claim to be God? And will Christianity stand up before twenty-first-century critics?[2]

When we doubt, we should confess our doubt to God as sin, we should study the evidence for the Christian faith, and we should test our own salvation.

3. Test your own salvation.

The apostle Paul tells us to test our faith. "Examine yourselves as to whether you are in faith. Prove yourselves. Do you not know yourselves, that Jesus Christ is in you?—unless indeed you are disqualified"(2 Corinthians 13:5).

This is what I did two years after I accepted Christ as Savior. The dialogue I had with myself went something like this:

What was your life like before you met Jesus? I asked myself.

I was dying inside, I replied.

How did you feel? I questioned further.

Full of pain, hopelessness, and fear, I answered.

Are things better now?

Much. When I received Jesus, I started to feel better, I answered.

Your experience with the Lord was real? I asked.

Well, yes, I think so.

Then what's your problem?

Think about your own life as you answer the questions below:
What was your life like before you met Jesus?

Are things better now? _____ yes _____ no
How?

Then what's your problem?
The real proof for our faith lies within ourselves. I know Jesus is real because I feel His presence within me. I've felt Him reach out to me when I pray, when I worship Him as I sing praise songs, when I get an answer to a question that is puzzling me—one that I know didn't come directly from my own knowledge. I also know the difference He has made in my life.

4. *Study the Word of God.*
The apostle Paul spent much of his adult life helping Christians grow spiritually. And he was very clear about the source of our faith. "Faith comes by hearing," he said, "and hearing by the word of God" (Romans 10:17). Reading the Word daily, regularly submitting to Bible teaching, and speaking the Word aloud will build our faith. Our mouths and hearts have to be united in this. One can't be saying, "God can," while the other says, "God can't." Our minds will convince our hearts as we read or speak God's Word.

And we must be careful to master the doctrines or basic teachings of the Bible if we are to be stable, mature Christians. In his first letter to his disciple Timothy, Paul advised him, "Till I come, give attention to reading, to exhortation, to doctrine . . . Take heed to yourself and to the doctrine. Continue in them, for in doing this you will save both yourself and those who hear you" (1 Timothy 4:13, 16). And he repeated this emphasis on basic teachings in his second letter to Timothy. "All Scripture is given by inspiration of God, and is profitable for doctrine, for reproof, for correction, for instruction in righteousness that the man of God may be complete, thoroughly equipped for every good work" (2 Timothy 3:16–17).

You might want to look for books that illuminate the basics of the Christian faith, like Max Anders's We Believe Series, which I quoted in Chapter 5.

As I look back on times when I sometimes doubted the Lord, I believe they occurred in busy or stressful moments when I had not spent enough time in the Word of God or had neglected being alone with the Lord in prayer and praise.

5. Pray.

The surest way to face doubts when they come is to have an extensive past history of answered prayer. I have included a prayer journal at the back of this book so that you can keep a record of your petitions and God's answers. Build your faith by referring to this journal every so often.

Faith is the key to the Christian life—and God's blessings. Scripture asserts: "Let him ask in faith, with no doubting, for he who doubts is like a wave of the sea driven and tossed by the wind. For let not that man suppose that he will receive anything from the Lord; he is a double-minded man, unstable in all his ways" (James 1:6–8).

Now as we end this chapter on faith, write a prayer asking God to strengthen your faith. You might want this to be a weekly part of your prayer time. And definitely write the same prayer in your journal at the end of this book. Then watch as God works in the days ahead to strengthen your faith in Him.

BIBLICAL STORIES OF FAITH

The Scripture passages below tell stories of faith. Often the event occurs in several books of the Bible. Read each version, then answer the questions.

Matthew 8:5–10

Who was healed?

Who had faith for the healing?

What was a distinguishing characteristic of this faith?

Matthew 9:1–8 (This story is also in Mark 2:1–12 and Luke 5:17–26.)

Who was healed?

Who had faith for the healing?

What was a distinguishing characteristic of this faith?

Matthew 15:21–28

Who was healed?

Who had faith for the healing?

What was a distinguishing characteristic of this faith?

Mark 5:25–34 (This story is also in Matthew 9:20–22 and Luke 8:43–48.)

Who was healed?

Who had faith for the healing?

What was a distinguishing characteristic of this faith?

Mark 5:35–43 (Also found in Matthew 9:23–26 and Luke 8:49–56)

Who was healed?

Who had faith for the healing?

What was a distinguishing characteristic of this faith?

Luke 18:35–43 (Also found in Matthew 20:29–34 and Mark 10:46–52)

Who was healed?

Who had faith for the healing?

What was a distinguishing characteristic of this faith?

Now that you have read these five events of faith, did you see any characteristics that are similar?

List these characteristics below:

CHAPTER TWENTY-TWO

Praying to Know How to Share Jesus

WHEN PEOPLE TELL ME ABOUT THEIR PROBLEMS, I TRY TO SHARE the love of Jesus with them since He has helped me through so many of my difficult times. One particular acquaintance, we'll call her Shelley, was continually telling me about her problems with her boyfriend and how miserable she was. She felt she had no purpose for her life.

"You know, you don't have to live in misery," I said one day.

"What do you mean?"

I told her how I used to be. "I was into drugs," I said, "alcohol, the occult. I used to be depressed all the time."

She couldn't believe it. "No, not *you*."

"Yes, it's true," I said. "I used to be so depressed I couldn't get out of bed. And now that's changed. God changed my life."

She looked at me skeptically, but still I continued. "The God I know isn't like any other god. All the other gods you read about—or hear people talking about—don't have any power to transform your life. My God does. Not only that, He has a purpose for your life. But you have to link up with Him. And the only way you can do that is to receive His Son."

I could tell that Shelley was listening to me, but she didn't seem to want to look directly into my eyes as I talked. Finally she said, "I'm afraid I'll have to give up some important things in my lifestyle if I believe in your God."

"Yes, you will," I admitted, "but God doesn't yank them away from you. He'll cause you to lose your taste for them. He doesn't just rip away something you're clinging to or loving. When He comes into your life—and you really repent of the way you have been living—He will change you from the inside out. No other god can do that."

It took several conversations like this, but Shelley seemed more receptive each time we talked. She also kept getting more and more miserable as time went on.

One day she was again elaborating on the problems she was having with her boyfriend. Her heart was very heavy.

"God can heal that hurt you're feeling," I said. "But you have to surrender your life to Him. He sets up a certain way for us to live, and we have to live His way. Once we do, He can pour all kinds of blessings into our lives."

"He can really get rid of the sadness I feel? The depression? The feelings of futility?"

"Yes, God will get rid of all that, but you have to give your whole life to Him."

She agreed to do that, and after she received the Lord, she started to cry. She had never before realized that the love of God was there for her.

Today Shelley has a wonderful husband and son. And she's happy for the first time in years. I see the fruit of the Lord in her life, but more important, she sees it too.

I feel Jesus was calling all of us when He gave His disciples the Great Commission. Hear Him speaking directly to you in these words from Matthew 28:19–20 and write your name in the blanks I have added.

Go therefore, _____, and make disciples of all the nations, baptizing them in the name of the Father and of the Son and of the Holy Spirit, teaching them to observe all things that I have commanded you, _____.

The Importance of Sharing Jesus

Let me give you four reasons why sharing Jesus is God's will for our lives.

1. All people are sinners.

The Bible is very blunt about this. Paul tells the Roman Christians, "There is none righteous, no, not one. There is none who understands. There is none who seeks after God. They have all gone out of the way" (Romans 3:10–12). The nice lady next door might be an obliging neighbor, but if she has not received Christ as Savior, she will not inherit eternal life.

2. Sharing Jesus is God's way of reaching those who do not know Him.

The apostle Paul asks all of us, "How then shall they call on Him in whom they have not believed? And how shall they believe in Him of whom they have not heard? And how shall they hear without a preacher?" (Romans 10:14–15). In this case we are all preachers. You see, your neighbor will only be saved if another human being witnesses to her. That could be you.

3. You cannot be certain that person will get another chance.

The story is told that D. L. Moody, the famous evangelist who founded Moody Bible Institute, always gave an altar call at the end of every sermon. He did so because he once ended a revival meeting in Chicago by telling the unbelievers to go home and seriously consider the claims of the gospel, then return on the following night prepared to make a decision for Christ. That night, October 8, 1871, the Chicago fire burned nearly four miles of the city, killing about 250 people. Moody always felt he had failed to fulfill God's great commission to these people.

Your neighbor might never have another chance to receive Christ if you don't talk to her now.

4. You are a Christian because someone shared Jesus with to you.

I would not be a Christian if some Christian singers who worked with me at one recording session had not shared Jesus with me and lived out their faith each day as we worked together. How about you? Who told you about Jesus? Your mom or dad? A girlfriend or boyfriend? Don't you suppose that Christ is expecting you to pass on this gift of eternal life to someone you know?

I know you're probably asking, "How? How do I do that?" Certainly I asked that question once I realized that Jesus was calling me to share my faith with other people.

ESSENTIAL WITNESSING TOOLS

Our witness will not be heard if we don't remember five important prerequisites.

1. Our lifestyle must reflect our Savior's.

People often say they don't go to church because of the "hypocrites" they meet there, i.e., the people who do not "walk the walk" of Christ. We cannot be a true witness for the Lord if we do not live according to His commandments.

King David knew this. After he confessed his adultery with Bathsheba, he pleaded with God, "Restore to me the joy of Your salvation, and uphold me with Your generous Spirit. Then I will teach transgressors Your ways, and sinners shall be converted to You" (Psalm 51:12–13). David knew that he could not reach out to sinners until he was living a clean lifestyle.

2. We must share simple facts, not profound theological concepts.

Leighton Ford, a well-known evangelist and Billy Graham's brother-in-law, wrote a book, *The Power of Story: Rediscovering the Oldest, Most Natural Way*, in which he advised others to "tell their stories." That, he said, was the significant way to reach other people for Christ. In other words, tell who you were before you were saved (just as I told Shelley) and how Christ changed your life (I gave up my old lifestyle and now I have wonderful children and a faithful husband; God has also given me a ministry to help others understand the power of prayer).[1]

There is no better witness than the difference Christ has made in our own lives.

3. We should avoid arguments and stick to the basics.

Those basics are: We are all sinners, we have all fallen short of the glory of God, and we all need a Savior so we can be reconciled to a sinless God. Christ died for our sins so that we may be made perfect in God's sight.

Sometimes an unbeliever will try to sidestep the gospel by asking questions like, How can I believe in a loving God when He allows _____? The person might mention the death of a loved one or a tragedy like the 2001 attack on the World Trade Center in New York City.

It's best to stay away from a theological discussion if possible. Later you can give the person a good book on this issue, like Philip Yancey's *Where Is God When It Hurts?* or James Dobson's *When God Doesn't Make Sense.*

4. We should use the Word of God.

The worksheet at the end of this chapter goes through the Scriptures that can be used to present the gospel. You can work through these Scriptures, then select the specific Scriptures that you would like to use and the way you want to use them. Beside each passage, note the next passage. Your Bible then becomes the map you use to work through the plan of salvation. Once you have talked through this process a few times to yourself, you should be able to present the gospel without referring to your notes.

5. We must depend upon the Spirit of God.

We tend to think that the apostles were eloquent speakers, so how could anyone resist their presentation of the gospel? Scripture tells us differently. The apostle Paul was very realistic about his own speaking ability. He told the Corinthians, "And my speech and my preaching were not with persuasive words of human wisdom, but in demonstration of the Spirit and of power, that your faith should not be in the wisdom of men but in the power of God" (1 Corinthians 2:3–5).

And when Stephen was brought before the council for speaking blasphemous words against Moses and God, the members of the council "were not able to resist the wisdom and the Spirit by which he spoke" (Acts 6:10). Note the Spirit's important role here. We must count on the Holy Spirit to be part of our exchange with our neighbor. And we should not expect to be eloquent in our presentation.

We should never allow our own assessment of our eloquence to keep us from speaking to our neighbor. We must count on God's Spirit to help us reach her. And we cannot be upset if she does not accept Christ as Savior at that moment. Again we must count on God's Spirit. Maybe we have just planted a seed that will be watered by someone else.

Stop now to write a prayer, asking the Lord to help you reach out to someone who needs to know Him. Mention that person by name and ask God to show you the best way to witness.

And now that you have pledged to bring another person to Christ, hear Him speaking the rest of the Great Commission to you directly. Again fill in the blank I have created with your own name. The Lord meant this promise for you:

And lo, I am with you always, _____, even to the end of the age.

FOUR STEPS TO WITNESSING

Here are the four steps that need to be taken if someone is to accept Christ as Savior. Look up the Scriptures below each step and write them in the blank spaces. Then check the Scripture that you feel is most useful to you.

1. God's Word says we are all sinners, condemned to hell.
   Isaiah 53:6

   Romans 3:10–11, 23

   Romans 5:8

   Revelation 20:15

2. A lost person can do nothing to save himself or herself.
   Isaiah 64:6

   Ephesians 2:9

3. Christ was born, crucified, and resurrected to save lost people from their sin.
   John 3:16

   1 Timothy 1:15

4. To be saved, a sinner must believe God's Word and invite Christ into his heart
   by faith.
   John 5:24

   Acts 16:31

Now go through your Bible and mark the passages you intend to use. Beside
each passage, note the next passage. Your Bible then becomes the map you use
to work through the plan of salvation.

CHAPTER TWENTY-THREE

Praying to Find Comfort in the Center of God's Will

BEING IN THE CENTER OF GOD'S WILL IS NOT ALWAYS COMFORTABLE. After we moved from California to Tennessee, we were miserable for the first year. I began to question if we had actually heard God when we made that decision. I asked God to confirm it again to me, and He did. When the house we lived in was destroyed in an earthquake not long after we moved from California, we all knew it was the Lord's will that we were not living there at that time. We never again questioned whether it was God's will to make that move.

The center of God's will is not a destination; it's the process itself. It won't always feel good, and it can, in fact, feel terrible. But as we choose to follow Him closely, to seek an intimate relationship with Him, to lay a solid foundation in His Word, and to walk obediently in His way, He keeps us in the center of His will.

The New Open Bible says that the greatest proof of the new birth is a changed life.[1] When you are in God's will, your life will be changed. *The New Open Bible* gives seven evidences of a changed life. I'm going to turn those into a quiz, which you can use to evaluate your journey in the next days and years. If you think you are wavering in your commitment to the Lord, take this quiz as an evaluation. Paul says, "Examine yourself as to whether you are in the faith. Prove yourselves" (2 Corinthians 13:5).

SEVEN EVIDENCES OF A CHANGED LIFE

1. A Love of Jesus
Do you have deep love for Jesus? Describe how you feel below:

2. A Love of the Bible
We will love God's Word as the psalmist does in Psalm 119. He cries out, "Behold, I long for Your precepts. Revive me in Your righteousness" (v. 40). And he expresses his great love for God's Word seventeen times in this psalm, which is an acrostic in praise of the Scriptures (see verses 24, 40, 47, 48, 72, 97, 103, 111, 113, 127, 129, 140, 143, 159, 162, 165, and 168).

Do you rejoice at God's Word as one who finds great treasure? What is one particular time in the last week when you have read the Bible and applied it to your life?

3. A Love for Other Christians
In John's letter to the early Christians in Asia he tells them, "We know that we have passed from death to life, because we love the brethren" (1 John 3:14).

Do you love the other members of Christ's community? _____ yes _____ no Mention those who have been especially meaningful to you in the last week or month:

4. A Love of Our Enemies
In Christ's Sermon on the Mount, He said, "You have heard that it was said, 'You shall love your neighbor and hate your enemy.' But I say to you, love your

enemies, bless those who curse you, do good to those who hate you, and pray for those who spitefully use you and persecute you, that you may be sons of your Father in heaven" (Matthew 5:43–45).

Have you been able to love your enemies in the last week? The last month? If not, write a prayer below that asks your Father to help you to love the specific person or persons who provoke you:

5. A Concern for the Souls of All People

Like Paul, we cry out for the conversion of our loved ones. Paul told the Roman Christians, "Brethren, my heart's desire and prayer to God for Israel is that they may be saved" (Romans 10:1).

A friend of mine serves on the board of directors for an international missionary society. One day when the board was interviewing prospective candidates, my friend asked a candidate whose parents were not Christians, "How do your mother and father feel about your leaving home and going so far away to serve Jesus?"

The young woman started to explain that her parents believed in God, just not Jesus, and that they hadn't objected to her becoming a missionary. But she never finished the statement because tears filled her eyes and she began to cry softly. "I sometimes wonder," she said, "why I am going so far away to bring people to Christ, when my mom and dad and my sisters and brothers do not believe in Him!"

My friend was upset that she had caused the young girl to cry, but she—and the rest of the mission board—knew that the candidate truly loved Jesus with all her heart and soul and mind because she wanted this for her family more than anything else.

Do you have a desire to see your loved ones and friends and acquaintances saved? If so, write how you might facilitate that in the next week or month:

6. A Love for the Pure Life

In Chapter 16 I mentioned that John says if we love the world, the love of the Father is not in us (1 John 2:15–17). Go over the list I gave you in that chapter and see how you are doing today:

- Do I judge myself by the world's standards for beauty, acceptability, and success? _____ yes _____ no
- Do I depend on worldly magazines and books to tell me how to live? _____ yes _____ no
- Am I willing to ignore certain convictions I have in order to find favor with other people? _____ yes _____ no
- Am I drawn toward emulating the lifestyles of celebrities rather than becoming who God created *me* to be? _____ yes _____ no
- Am I willing to compromise what I know of God's ways in order to gain something I want? _____ yes _____ no

If you said yes to any of these questions, you are cutting off the possibilities God has for your life. Write a prayer below asking God to help you turn your eyes away from the world and on to the Lord.

7. A Yearning to Talk with God

Paul describes living in the spirit as "speaking to one another in psalms and hymns and spiritual songs, singing and making melody in your heart to the Lord" (Ephesians 5:19).

Do you yearn to talk with your Father daily? If so, write a prayer below, asking Him to help you set aside a specific time each day to do so:

A Short Quiz

You might want to take this test once a week in the shortened version below to see if you are in the center of God's will for your life.

1. Do you love Jesus with all your heart and soul and mind?

2. Do you read the Bible daily—and enjoy doing so?

3. Do you love other Christians in your church and in your community?

4. Do you love those who have frustrated or harmed you in the last week?

5. Do you wish to reach out to loved ones and friends and those you meet casually who do not have a saving faith?

6. Have you conducted yourself in the last week in a way that would glorify your Savior?

7. Have you talked with your Father and heard Him speak to you?

Finding God's will for your life comes about by taking steps every day to live in His will as revealed by His Word. As you think about your life now, what do you think God's will is for you during the next week? Write that in the space below:

What is His will for you in the next month?

In the next year?

Five years from now?

Look back to page 7 in Chapter 1. Compare your thoughts then to your current evaluation. Have they changed? If so, write how in the space below.

Now look toward the future. John told the early Christians, "The world is passing away, and the lust of it; but he who does the will of God abides forever" (1 John 2:17). And Paul continually pleaded with God for his converts in Asia: "For this reason we also, since the day we heard it, do not cease to pray for you, and to ask that you may be filled with the knowledge of His will in all wisdom and spiritual understanding; that you may have a walk worthy of the Lord, fully pleasing Him, being fruitful in every good work and increasing in the knowledge of God" (Colossians 1:9–10).

Write a prayer below asking the Lord to walk with you in this way:

And then look toward the day when you will meet Him at the end of your journey here on earth. None of us know just exactly what this moment will be like, but God describes it this way: "Eye has not seen, nor ear heard, nor have entered into the heart of man the things which God has prepared for those who love Him" (1 Corinthians 2:9).

God has more for you than you can ever dream of. And you find this by walking in obedience, which is the will of God.

Read Your Bible Through in a Year

A systematic division of the books of the Bible, primarily for reading.

JANUARY

MATT. (Morning) / GEN. (Evening)

Date	Morning	Evening
1	1	1, 2, 3
2	2	4, 5, 6
3	3	7, 8, 9
4	4	10, 11, 12
5	5: 1-26	13, 14, 15
6	5: 27-48	16, 17
7	6: 1-18	18, 19
8	6: 19-34	20, 21, 22
9	7	23, 24
10	8: 1-17	25, 26
11	8: 18-34	27, 28
12	9: 1-17	29, 30
13	9: 18-38	31, 32
14	10: 1-20	33, 34, 35
15	10: 21-42	36, 37, 38
16	11	39, 40
17	12: 1-23	41, 42
18	12: 24-50	43, 44, 45
19	13: 1-30	46, 47, 48
20	13: 31-58	49, 50
		EX.
21	14: 1-21	1, 2, 3
22	14: 22-36	4, 5, 6
23	15: 1-20	7, 8
24	15: 21-39	9, 10, 11
25	16	12, 13
26	17	14, 15
27	18: 1-20	16, 17, 18
28	18: 21-35	19, 20
29	19	21, 22
30	20: 1-16	23, 24
31	20: 17-34	25, 26

FEBRUARY

MATT. (Morning) / EX. (Evening)

Date	Morning	Evening
1	21: 1-22	27, 28
2	21: 23-46	29, 30
3	22: 1-22	31, 32, 33
4	22: 23-46	34, 35
5	23: 1-22	36, 37, 38
6	23: 23-39	39, 40
		LEV.
7	24: 1-28	1, 2, 3
8	24: 29-51	4, 5
9	25: 1-30	6, 7
10	25: 31-46	8, 9, 10
11	26: 1-25	11, 12
12	26: 26-50	13
13	26: 51-75	14
14	27: 1-26	15, 16
15	27: 27-50	17, 18
16	27: 51-66	19, 20
17	28	21, 22
	MARK	
18	1: 1-22	23, 24
19	1: 23-45	25
20	2	26, 27
		NUM.
21	3: 1-19	1, 2
22	3: 20-35	3, 4
23	4: 1-20	5, 6
24	4: 21-41	7, 8
25	5: 1-20	9, 10, 11
26	5: 21-43	12, 13, 14
27	6: 1-29	15, 16
28	6: 30-56	17, 18, 19
29	7: 1-13	20, 21, 22

MARCH

MARK (Morning) / NUM. (Evening)

Date	Morning	Evening
1	7: 14-37	23, 24, 25
2	8: 1-21	26, 27
3	8: 22-38	28, 29, 30
4	9: 1-29	31, 32, 33
5	9: 30-50	34, 35, 36
		DUT.
6	10: 1-31	1, 2
7	10: 32-52	3, 4
8	11: 1-18	5, 6, 7
9	11: 19-33	8, 9, 10
10	12: 1-27	11, 12, 13
11	12: 28-44	14, 15, 16
12	13: 1-20	17, 18, 19
13	13: 21-37	20, 21, 22
14	14: 1-26	23, 24, 25
15	14: 27-53	26, 27
16	14: 54-72	28, 29
17	15: 1-25	30, 31
18	15: 26-47	32, 33, 34
		JOSH.
19	16	1, 2, 3
	LUKE	
20	1: 1-20	4, 5, 6
21	1: 21-38	7, 8, 9
22	1: 39-56	10, 11, 12
23	1: 57-80	13, 14, 15
24	2: 1-24	16, 17, 18
25	2: 25-52	19, 20, 21
26	3	22, 23, 24
		JUDG.
27	4: 1-30	1, 2, 3
28	4: 31-44	4, 5, 6
29	5: 1-16	7, 8
30	5: 17-39	9, 10
31	6: 1-26	11, 12

APRIL

LUKE (Morning) / JUDG. (Evening)

Date	Morning	Evening
1	6: 27-49	13, 14, 15
2	7: 1-30	16, 17, 18
3	7: 31-50	19, 20, 21
		RUTH
4	8: 1-25	1, 2, 3, 4
		1 SAM.
5	8: 26-56	1, 2, 3
6	9: 1-17	4, 5, 6
7	9: 18-36	7, 8, 9
8	9: 37-62	10, 11, 12
9	10: 1-24	13, 14
10	10: 25-42	15, 16
11	11: 1-28	17, 18
12	11: 29-54	19, 20, 21
13	12: 1-31	22, 23, 24
14	12: 32-59	25, 26
15	13: 1-22	27, 28, 29
16	13: 23-35	30, 31
		2 SAM.
17	14: 1-24	1, 2
18	14: 25-35	3, 4, 5
19	15: 1-10	6, 7, 8
20	15: 11-32	9, 10, 11
21	16	12, 13
22	17: 1-19	14, 15
23	17: 20-37	16, 17, 18
24	18: 1-23	19, 20
25	18: 24-43	21, 22
26	19: 1-27	23, 24
		1 KIN.
27	19: 28-48	1, 2
28	20: 1-23	3, 4, 5
29	20: 27-47	6, 7
30	21: 1-19	8, 9

MAY

LUKE (Morning) / 1 KIN. (Evening)

Date	Morning	Evening
1	21: 20-38	10, 11
2	22: 1-20	12, 13
3	22: 21-46	14, 15
4	22: 47-71	16, 17, 18
5	23: 1-25	19, 20
6	23: 26-56	21, 22
		2 KIN.
7	24: 1-35	1, 2, 3
8	24: 36-53	4, 5, 6
	JOHN	
9	1: 1-28	7, 8, 9
10	1: 29-51	10, 11, 12
11	2	13, 14
12	3: 1-18	15, 16
13	3: 19-38	17, 18
14	4: 1-30	19, 20, 21
15	4: 31-54	22, 23
16	5: 1-24	24, 25
		1 CHR.
17	5: 25-47	1, 2, 3
18	6: 1-21	4, 5, 6
19	6: 22-44	7, 8, 9
20	6: 45-71	10, 11, 12
21	7: 1-27	13, 14, 15
22	7: 28-53	16, 17, 18
23	8: 1-27	19, 20, 21
24	8: 28-59	22, 23, 24
25	9: 1-23	25, 26, 27
26	9: 24-41	28, 29
		2 CHR.
27	10: 1-23	1, 2, 3
28	10: 24-42	4, 5, 6
29	11: 1-29	7, 8, 9
30	11: 30-57	10, 11, 12
31	12: 1-26	13, 14

JUNE

JOHN (Morning) / 2 CHR. (Evening)

Date	Morning	Evening
1	12: 27-50	15, 16
2	13: 1-20	17, 18
3	13: 21-38	19, 20
4	14	21, 22
5	15	23, 24
6	16	25, 26, 27
7	17	28, 29
8	18: 1-18	30, 31
9	18: 19-40	32, 33
10	19: 1-22	34, 35, 36
		EZRA
11	19: 23-42	1, 2
12	20	3, 4, 5
13	21	6, 7, 8
	ACTS	
14	1	9, 10
		NEH.
15	2: 1-21	1, 2, 3
16	2: 22-47	4, 5, 6
17	3	7, 8, 9
18	4: 1-22	10, 11
19	4: 23-37	12, 13
		ESTH.
20	5: 1-21	1, 2
21	5: 22-42	3, 4, 5
22	6	6, 7, 8
23	7: 1-21	9, 10
		JOB
24	7: 22-43	1, 2
25	7: 44-60	3, 4
26	8: 1-25	5, 6, 7
27	8: 26-40	8, 9, 10
28	9: 1-21	11, 12, 13
29	9: 22-43	14, 15, 16
30	10: 1-23	17, 18, 19

JULY

Date	Morning	Evening
1	ACTS 10:24-48	JOB 20, 21
2	11	22, 23, 24
3	12	25, 26, 27
4	13: 1-25	28, 29
5	13:26-52	30, 31
6	14	32, 33
7	15: 1-21	34, 35
8	15:22-41	36, 37
9	16: 1-21	38, 39, 40
10	16:22-40	41, 42
11	17: 1-15	PS. 1, 2, 3
12	17:16-34	4, 5, 6
13	18	7, 8, 9
14	19: 1-20	10, 11, 12
15	19:21-41	13, 14, 15
16	20: 1-16	16, 17
17	20:17-38	18, 19
18	21: 1-17	20, 21, 22
19	21:18-40	23, 24, 25
20	22	26, 27, 28
21	23: 1-15	29, 30
22	23:16-35	31, 32
23	24	33, 34
24	25	35, 36
25	26	37, 38, 39
26	27: 1-26	40, 41, 42
27	27:27-44	43, 44, 45
28	28	46, 47, 48
29	ROM. 1	49, 50
30	2	51, 52, 53
31	3	54, 55, 56

AUGUST

Date	Morning	Evening
1	ROM. 4	PS. 57, 58, 59
2	5	60, 61, 62
3	6	63, 64, 65
4	7	66, 67
5	8: 1-21	68, 69
6	8:22-39	70, 71
7	9: 1-15	72, 73
8	9:16-33	74, 75, 76
9	10	77, 78
10	11: 1-18	79, 80
11	11:19-36	81, 82, 83
12	12	84, 85, 86
13	13	87, 88
14	14	89, 90
15	15: 1-13	91, 92, 93
16	15:14-33	94, 95, 96
17	16	97, 98, 99
18	1 COR. 1	100, 101, 102
19	2	103, 104
20	3	105, 106
21	4	107, 108, 109
22	5	110, 111, 112
23	6	113, 114, 115
24	7: 1-19	116, 117, 118
25	7:20-40	119: 1-88
26	8	119: 89-176
27	9	120, 121, 122
28	10: 1-18	123, 124, 125
29	10:19-33	126, 127, 128
30	11: 1-16	129, 130, 131
31	11:17-34	132, 133, 134

SEPTEMBER

Date	Morning	Evening
1	1 COR. 12	PS. 135, 136
2	13	137, 138, 139
3	14: 1-20	140, 141, 142
4	14:21-40	143, 144, 145
5	15: 1-28	146, 147
6	15:29-58	148, 149, 150
7	16	PROV. 1, 2
8	2 COR. 1	3, 4, 5
9	2	6, 7
10	3	8, 9
11	4	10, 11, 12
12	5	13, 14, 15
13	6	16, 17, 18
14	7	19, 20, 21
15	8	22, 23, 24
16	9	25, 26
17	10	27, 28, 29
18	11: 1-15	30, 31
19	11:16-33	ECCL. 1, 2, 3
20	12	4, 5, 6
21	13	7, 8, 9
22	GAL. 1	10, 11, 12
23	2	SONG 1, 2, 3
24	3	4, 5
25	4	6, 7, 8
26	5	IS. 1, 2
27	6	3, 4
28	EPH. 1	5, 6
29	2	7, 8
30	3	9, 10

OCTOBER

Date	Morning	Evening
1	EPH. 4	IS. 11, 12, 13
2	5: 1-16	14, 15, 16
3	5:17-33	17, 18, 19
4	6	20, 21, 22
5	PHIL. 1	23, 24, 25
6	2	26, 27
7	3	28, 29
8	4	30, 31
9	COL. 1	32, 33
10	2	34, 35, 36
11	3	37, 38
12	4	39, 40
13	1 THESS. 1	41, 42
14	2	43, 44
15	3	45, 46
16	4	47, 48, 49
17	5	50, 51, 52
18	2 THESS. 1	53, 54, 55
19	2	56, 57, 58
20	3	59, 60, 61
21	1 TIM. 1	62, 63, 64
22	2	65, 66
23	3	JER. 1, 2
24	4	3, 4, 5
25	5	6, 7, 8
26	6	9, 10, 11
27	2 TIM. 1	12, 13, 14
28	2	15, 16, 17
29	3	18, 19
30	4	20, 21
31	TITUS 1	22, 23

NOVEMBER

Date	Morning	Evening
1	TITUS 2	JER. 24, 25, 26
2	3	27, 28, 29
3	PHILEM.	30, 31
4	HEB. 1	32, 33
5	2	34, 35, 36
6	3	37, 38, 39
7	4	40, 41, 42
8	5	43, 44, 45
9	6	46, 47
10	7	48, 49
11	8	50
12	9	51, 52
13	10: 1-18	LAM. 1, 2
14	10:19-39	3, 4, 5
15	11: 1-19	EZEK. 1, 2
16	11:20-40	3, 4
17	12	5, 6, 7
18	13	8, 9, 10
19	JAMES 1	11, 12, 13
20	2	14, 15
21	3	16, 17
22	4	18, 19
23	5	20, 21
24	1 PET. 1	22, 23
25	2	24, 25, 26
26	3	27, 28, 29
27	4	30, 31, 32
28	5	33, 34
29	2 PET. 1	35, 36
30	2	37, 38, 39

DECEMBER

Date	Morning	Evening
1	2 PET. 3	EZEK. 40, 41
2	1 JOHN 1	42, 43, 44
3	2	45, 46
4	3	47, 48
5	4	DAN. 1, 2
6	5	3, 4
7	2 JOHN	5, 6, 7
8	3 JOHN	8, 9, 10
9	JUDE	11, 12
10	REV. 1	HOS. 1, 2, 3, 4
11	2	5, 6, 7, 8
12	3	9, 10, 11
13	4	12, 13, 14
14	5	JOEL 1, 2, 3
15	6	AMOS 1, 2, 3
16	7	4, 5, 6
17	8	7, 8, 9
18	9	OBAD.
19	10	JON.
20	11	MIC. 1, 2, 3
21	12	4, 5
22	13	6, 7
23	14	NAH.
24	15	HAB.
25	16	ZEPH.
26	17	HAG.
27	18	ZECH. 1, 2, 3, 4
28	19	5, 6, 7, 8
29	20	9, 10, 11, 12
30	21	13, 14
31	22	MAL.

Notes

Chapter Two

1. C. S. Lewis, *The Screwtape Letters* (San Francisco: Harper, 2001).
2. James Strong, *Strong's Hebrew and Chaldee Dictionary*, "elohim," #430.
3. Ibid., "eloah," #433.

Chapter Three

1. James Bryan Smith, "Blessed Are the Feet: How Rich Changed My Life" (*Home Life Magazine*, August 2000).
2. Les Sussman, *Praise Him! Christian Music Stars Share Their Favorite Verses from the Scriptures* (Berkley, 1999).
3. Ibid.
4. Ibid.
5. Ibid.
6. Ibid.
7. Ibid.
8. Ibid.
9. Rich Mullins and Beaker, "Creed" (BMG Songs, Inc. 1993).
   CREED (Rich Mullins and Beaker) © 1993 BMG Songs, Inc. (ASCAP) and Kid Brothers of St. Frank Publishing (ASCAP). All rights on behalf of Kid Brothers of St. Frank Pub. Admin. by BMG Songs, Inc. (ASCAP). BMG MUSIC PUBLISHING controls100% worldwide.
10. Rich Mullins, "In His Own Words, Rich Mullins" (*CCM Magazine*, 1997).
11. Smith.

Chapter Four

1. Dr. Larry Stephens, *Please Let Me Know You, God* (Nashville: Thomas Nelson, 1993), 85–89.
2. Ibid., 135–138.

Chapter Five

1. Max Anders, *The Holy Spirit: Knowing Our Comforter* (Nashville: Thomas Nelson, 1995), 3.

2. Ibid., 33.

3. Ibid., 27–28.

4. J. Vernon McGee, *Thru the Bible, Matthew Through Romans* (Nashville: Thomas Nelson, 1983), 699.

5. Max Anders, *What You Need to Know About the Holy Spirit: 12 Lessons* (Nashville: Thomas Nelson, 1998), 51.

6. Ibid. 52.

Chapter Seven

1. These seven purposes for suffering are taken from the explanatory notes in *The New Open Bible* (Nashville: Thomas Nelson, 1985). Used by permission. Copyright © 1985 by Thomas Nelson, Inc.

2. Jodi Berndt, *Celebration of Miracles* (Nashville: Thomas Nelson, 1995), 6–7.

3. Ibid., 8–9.

4. Ibid., 12.

5. Ibid., 9–10.

6. Ibid., 10.

Chapter Nine

1. The twenty-two letters of the Hebrew alphabet are: *aleph, beth, gimel, daleth, he, vau, zain, cheth, teth, jod, caph, lamed, mem, nun, samech, ain, pe, tzaddi, koph, resh, schin,* and *tau.*

2. We will use the New Living Translation for this study.

3. From *The New Open Bible* (Nashville: Thomas Nelson, 1985), 1549–54. Used by permission. Copyright © 1985 by Thomas Nelson, Inc.

4. Josh McDowell, *The New Evidence That Demands a Verdict* (Nashville: Thomas Nelson, 1999), 61.

5. Ibid. 63.

6. Ibid.

7. Ibid. 77.

8. Ibid. 77–78.

9. Susman.

10. Ibid.

Chapter Ten

1. Lewis, 20.

2. Ibid. 21.

Chapter Eleven

1. Merlin R. Carothers, *Prison to Praise* (United States, 1970), 93. Used by permission. Merlin R. Carothers, Box 2518, Escondido, CA 92033.
2. Ibid.
3. Ibid.
4. Ibid.
5. Ibid. 94–95.
6. Strong, "hallelu," #239.
7. Carothers, 107.

Chapter Twelve

1. Strong, Peter," #4074.

Chapter Thirteen

1. Les Carter and Frank Minirth, *The Choosing to Forgive Workbook* (Nashville: Thomas Nelson, 1997), 47–49.
2. Ibid. 50.
3. Lewis, 16.

Chapter Fourteen

1. Oswald Chambers, *My Utmost for His Highest* (Westwood, N.J.: Barbour & Co., 1984), 151.
2. J. Vernon McGee, *Thru the Bible: 1 Corinthians Through Revelation* (Nashville: Thomas Nelson, 1983), 765.

Chapter Fifteen

1. McDowell, xxvi.
2. Strong, "sanctify," #37.
3. McDowell, xxvii.

Chapter Sixteen

1. Strong, "world," #2889.
2. Lewis, 132.
3. Ibid. 159.

Chapter Seventeen

1. McGee, *Thru the Bible, Matthew through Romans,* 683.
2. Ibid. 21.

Chapter Eighteen
1. Joni Eareckson Tada, *Ordinary People, Extraordinary Faith* (Nashville: Thomas Nelson, 2001), 5.
2. *Webster's New World College Dictionary, Third Edition* (New York: Simon & Schuster, 1997), "fellowship."
3. McGee, *Thru the Bible: 1 Corinthians through Revelation*, 126.
4. Lewis, 12.
5. Smith.
6. Lewis, 45–47.

Chapter Twenty
1. Smith.
2. McGee, *Thru the Bible: 1 Corinthians through Revelation*, 55.
3. Ibid.

Chapter Twenty-One
1. Lewis, 39.
2. McDowell.

Chapter Twenty-Two
1. Leighton Ford, *The Power of Story: Rediscovering the Oldest, Most Natural Way to Reach People for Christ* (Colorado Springs, CO: NavPress, 1994).

Chapter Twenty-Three
1. From *The New Open Bible* (Nashville: Thomas Nelson, 1985). Used by permission. Copyright © 1985 by Thomas Nelson, Inc.

About the Author

STORMIE OMARTIAN IS A POPULAR WRITER, ACCOMPLISHED LYRICIST, and speaker. She is the best-selling author of ten books, including *The Power of a Praying Wife, The Power of a Praying Husband, The Power of a Praying Parent, Lord, I Want to Be Whole,* and *Stormie,* the story of her journey from the brokenness of being an abused child to becoming a whole person.

A popular media guest, Stormie has appeared on numerous radio and television programs, including *The 700 Club, Parent Talk, Homelife, Crosstalk,* and *Today's Issues.* Stormie speaks all over the United States in churches, at women's retreats, and for conferences. For twenty years, Stormie has been encouraging women to pray for their families. She desires to help others become all that God created them to be, to establish strong family bonds and marriages, and to be instruments of God's love.

Stormie has been married to Grammy-winning record producer Michael Omartian for nearly thirty years. They have three grown children, Christopher, Amanda, and John David.

You can contact Stormie through her Web site:

www.stormieomartian.com

PRAYING GOD'S WILL FOR YOUR LIFE

"GOD, IF YOU HAVE A WILL FOR MY LIFE, I NEED TO KNOW WHAT IT is and what to do about it."

Even before she became a Christian, Stormie Omartian prayed those words. In the months that followed, God answered her in ways that she didn't believe possible. As God unfolded His plan for her life, she began to understand what it meant to live in God's will. And she found that she could share her discovery with other people.

Praying God's Will for Your Life is not a book about finding the right person to marry or deciding on a career. It is a book about a way of life and a heart attitude that are God's will for everyone who knows Him. That way of life encompasses three important components:

- An intimate relationship with God
- A solid foundation in God's truth
- A commitment to obedience

ISBN: 0-7852-6645-3

LORD, I WANT TO BE WHOLE

"LORD, I WANT TO BE WHOLE."

These words are the heart-cry of many Christians who, in spite of their relationship with the Lord, find themselves dealing with overwhelming anger, guilt, depression—or perhaps the nagging feeling that something inside them just is not right.

In *Lord, I Want to Be Whole,* Stormie Omartian shares the principles she learned during her struggle for real and lasting peace. What Stormie offers is not a formula for a quick fix but a positive approach that is both spiritual and practical. Her advice and encouragement will help you find—and keep—wholeness in all areas of your life.

ISBN: 0-7852-6703-4

CPSIA information can be obtained at www.ICGtesting.com
Printed in the USA
241923LV00001B/2/P

9 780785 264071